The Social Work Field Instructor's Survival Guide

Melissa A. Hensley, PhD, LISW, is an assistant professor of social work and field education coordinator at Augsburg College in Minneapolis, Minnesota. She earned a BA in history, an MSW, and a PhD in social work from the Brown School at Washington University in St. Louis, Missouri. In addition, she holds a master's degree in health administration from the University of Missouri–Columbia School of Medicine. Dr. Hensley has experience as a social work field instructor for several colleges and universities. In addition, she teaches the Integrative Field Seminar course for foundation-year MSW students at Augsburg College. Prior to her career in higher education, Dr. Hensley worked as a social worker in the fields of housing/homelessness services and community mental health. She is active as a volunteer in mental health policy advocacy and education.

The Social Work Field Instructor's Survival Guide

Melissa A. Hensley, PhD, LISW

Editor

SPRINGER PUBLISHING COMPANY
NEW YORK

Springer Publishing Company, LLC
11 West 42nd Street
New York, NY 10036
www.springerpub.com

Acquisitions Editor: Stephanie Drew
Composition: S4Carlisle Publishing Services

ISBN: 978-0-8261-2776-1
e-book ISBN: 978-0-8261-2777-8

15 16 17 18 19 / 5 4 3 2 1

The author and the publisher of this Work have made every effort to use sources believed to be reliable to provide information that is accurate and compatible with the standards generally accepted at the time of publication. The author and publisher shall not be liable for any special, consequential, or exemplary damages resulting, in whole or in part, from the readers' use of, or reliance on, the information contained in this book. The publisher has no responsibility for the persistence or accuracy of URLs for external or third-party Internet websites referred to in this publication and does not guarantee that any content on such websites is, or will remain, accurate or appropriate.

Library of Congress Cataloging-in-Publication Data

The social work field instructor's survival guide / Melissa A. Hensley, PhD, LISW, editor.
    pages cm
Includes index.
ISBN 978-0-8261-2776-1
1. Social service—Fieldwork. 2. Social work education. I. Hensley, Melissa, editor.
HV11.S588335 2016
361.3071'55—dc23
                                                                    2015029704

Printed in the United States of America by Gasch Printing.

This book is dedicated to the memory of Dr. Annette Gerten, associate professor of social work and BSW field education director at Augsburg College from 1996 until her death from an aggressive cancer in 2013. Dr. Gerten served as a role model for faculty, field instructors, and students alike in her commitment to quality teaching and ethical social work practice.

Contents

Contributors

Laura A. Boisen, PhD, LICSW
Professor of Social Work
MSW Field Education
  Coordinator
Augsburg College
Minneapolis, Minnesota

Lois Bosch, PhD, LISW
Professor of Social Work
MSW Program Director
Augsburg College
Minneapolis, Minnesota

Mary Simonson Clark, BS-OT,
  MA/MSW, LGSW
Freelance Writer
Field Instructor, Department of
  Social Work
Augsburg College
Minneapolis, Minnesota

Christina L. Erickson, PhD, LISW
Associate Professor of Social
  Work
BSW Field Education
  Coordinator
Augsburg College
Minneapolis, Minnesota

Melissa A. Hensley, PhD, LISW
Assistant Professor of Social
  Work
Field Education Coordinator
Augsburg College
Minneapolis, Minnesota

Bibiana Koh, PhD, LICSW
Assistant Professor of Social Work
BSW Program Coordinator
Augsburg College
Minneapolis, Minnesota

Preface

Field education has been identified as the "signature pedagogy" of social work education (Wayne, Bogo, & Raskin, 2010). The practice of having students working alongside community practitioners is almost as old as the social work profession itself (Reamer, 2012). Students who study social work not only need to possess excellent intellectual and academic skills, but they also need to be able to translate classroom knowledge into effective practice in the real-world settings where social work takes place (Rosenberg, 2009). Field education, which involves students working with practicing social workers to learn the knowledge, skills, and values of the social work profession, brings the intellectual content of the classroom into focus with everyday tasks and responsibilities.

Therefore, the work of community-based practitioners—field instructors—who supervise social work interns is essential to our profession. Without the many hours that practicing social workers spend training, monitoring, and assisting students, our profession could not advance.

Despite the critical role that community-based supervisors play in the training of social work students, there are not enough resources available for social work field instructors. Although individual college and university social work programs offer some training for practitioners who supervise students, there is a need for a source of information that can provide guidance across specific field education programs. Specific social work departments or schools may have policies that are unique to their programs, but there are many aspects of the field education process that are relatively consistent across schools. In addition, although field education directors from social work programs work hard to be available and helpful to field instructors, it would be useful for field instructors to have a guidebook of their own, which they can consult when general questions arise.

This is the purpose of this book—to serve as a source of information regarding social work field instruction, to which practicum supervisors can turn when questions or challenges arise. This volume includes content on how to recruit a practicum student, as well as useful information about effective supervision, learning assessment planning and development, integration of theory and practice, helpful evaluation techniques, and teaching social work ethics. It is designed to provide an introduction to the practice of field education, along with useful recommendations about how to maximize the learning experience of practicum students.

The contributors to this volume are educators from a social work department at a midwestern liberal arts college. All of us had many years of practice experience prior to joining academia. We have been practicum students, clinical and community social workers, field instructors, classroom instructors, field seminar leaders, and administrators. We hope to share with you the basics of effective field instruction, along with knowledge and skills that will help you excel in your role of educating the future generations of the social work profession.

Melissa A. Hensley

REFERENCES

Reamer, F. (2012). Essential ethics education in social work field education. *Field Educator*, 2(2). Retrieved March 14, 2015, from http://www.fieldeducator.simmons.edu/article/essential-ethics-education-in-social-work-field-instruction

Rosenberg, J. (2009). *Working in social work: The real world guide to practice settings.* New York, NY: Routledge.

Wayne, J., Bogo, M., & Raskin, M. (2010, Fall). Field education as the signature pedagogy of social work education. *Journal of Social Work Education*, 46(3), 327–339.

Acknowledgments

The editor and contributors would like to acknowledge the support of Dr. Michael Schock, chair of the Augsburg College Social Work Department, as well as all of the members of the department faculty, for their support of and belief in this project. Dr. Hensley would also like to thank Dr. Lori Peterson, former dean of graduate and professional studies at Augsburg College, for her ongoing encouragement.

Most of all, the editor and contributors acknowledge the hard work and generous contributions of all of the field instructors who are affiliated with the Augsburg College BSW and MSW programs. We could not do our work without you!

ONE

Working With a Practicum Student: First Steps

Melissa A. Hensley

Field education (the practicum) is an integral aspect of every social work student's training. Whether a student is obtaining a bachelor's degree in social work (BSW) in the hope of pursuing a career in generalist practice or working toward a master's degree in social work (MSW) to prepare for advanced or independent work, learning skills and practice techniques in community settings is essential. The work that is performed by students in the field is supervised by social workers in many different organizational and practice settings. These social workers, also known as field instructors, serve as mentors and guides throughout students' practicum experiences. The relationship between the field instructor and the social work student provides fertile ground for socialization as a member of a profession and the acquisition of practice skills (Weiss, Gal, & Cnaan, 2008). The social work field could not develop and grow without the generous contribution of field instructors to the educational process.

Being a field instructor benefits the practitioner as well. Interaction with students, staff, and faculty members from a social work program helps the practitioner pursue the ethical value of lifelong learning that is an essential part of the National Association of Social Workers (NASW) *Code of Ethics* (Ward & Mama, 2010). Serving as a field instructor also keeps supervisory skills fresh and provides a way for professionals to give back to their profession and the community.

HOW DO I BECOME A FIELD INSTRUCTOR?

If you are a social worker with at least 2 years of practice experience, you may be eligible to serve as a field instructor for a college or university social work program. Some states may also require that social work field instructors hold a state license to practice social work.

If your agency currently hosts practicum students, but you have not served as a field instructor, talk to your organization's program manager or training coordinator. These individuals can help you with the process of becoming a field instructor at your agency.

If your agency does not currently host practicum students, you can contact BSW and MSW programs at local universities in order to learn about the process necessary for your agency to become a practicum site. This will usually involve providing basic information about your agency and the kinds of tasks and activities in which students would be engaged. If you will be the field instructor for your agency, you may be expected to submit a résumé and describe your educational background and work experience.

WHAT IF I'D LIKE TO HAVE A PRACTICUM STUDENT BUT I DON'T CURRENTLY HAVE ONE?

The process by which students choose their practica varies greatly from program to program. On one end of the spectrum, students may have free reign to investigate various opportunities, and to apply and interview at agencies that interest them. On the other end, social work programs may have a matching system in which students list their top choices and are matched with agencies that are willing to accept them. You will want to be familiar with the processes at colleges and universities that place students at your worksite.

Some colleges and universities hold "field fair" events, which are attended by agencies interested in having practicum students as well as social work students. These events provide an opportunity for students to learn more about practicum placement opportunities and to meet representatives from those agencies. If you are interested in having a student in your setting, these events can be helpful for identifying potential candidates.

You will also want to make sure that all of the colleges and universities that could potentially provide a practicum student have up-to-date information about your organization's staff, the designated field instructors, and the kinds of learning opportunities that your agency can provide. When schools send e-mails or other requests for updated information, it is important to respond promptly and provide any needed updates—this will help ensure that the college or university can help you connect with a student who is best suited to the opportunities you can provide. Some agencies develop job descriptions for internship positions that they send to college/university social work programs. Such job descriptions can be especially helpful when an agency is seeking a student to fulfill a particular role within a program or service.

> **Case Example:** Recovery Partners, a local counseling and community mental health agency, had served as a site for MSW clinical-concentration students for many years. However, the Recovery Partners development and marketing director, who herself possessed an MSW, wanted to recruit a community practice intern to help with outreach and the development of a strategic plan for the agency. The development and marketing director developed a specific job description for this practicum experience, using her knowledge of expected social work competencies. She shared this job description with the MSW field

directors in the area, and within a few weeks, she was able to interview several students and select a student for the community practice internship opportunity.

Certain other requirements also exist. Agencies hosting social work practicum students must be familiar with and adhere to the NASW *Code of Ethics*. In addition, agencies that train social work students should have a comprehensive nondiscrimination policy in place (Birkenmaier, 2011).

The selection process for bringing a practicum student into your agency should include some of the same elements that would be used in a job search for an open staff position. Potential interns should be interviewed to ensure that their existing skill sets and academic/ professional interests fit well with the mission and program activities of the agency. Because students are still learning the social work profession, they may not possess a full complement of practice skills, but they should at least demonstrate a positive work ethic and show the potential for development of effective communication and other practice skills (Ward & Mama, 2010).

PRACTICUM AND INTERNSHIP ROLES

If you are considering having a social work practicum student as an intern at your organization, there are several points to keep in mind before affiliating with a college or university's field education program. First, are you interested in having an undergraduate or graduate student work at your organization? Bachelor of Social Work students may possess a different skill set than graduate students. In addition, the students' grade level (Junior or Senior, for undergraduate, or Foundation or Concentration, for graduate students) may affect the skills they bring to the practicum as well as their own needs and expectations. Second, what role will the intern play? Is there a particular program with which you'd like to place a student, or will the student be shadowing and working with a number of different programs? Third, do you have the time and energy to devote to the expectations of field instruction? Having an intern to help out with agency tasks can be a time saver in some ways, but students need consistent, adequate supervision and mentoring in order to have a successful practicum experience. If you cannot commit to providing regular one-on-one time for supervision, as well as other training and mentoring tasks, then you should not take on a practicum student.

You will also want to consider what kinds of tasks at the agency would be suitable for a practicum student—will your agency provide strong training in generalist direct-practice and community-practice skills? Is your agency more suited to the learning expectations of clinical-practice or macro-practice students? What kinds of work will interns participate in? Do you have enough appropriate tasks and activities to keep a practicum student occupied? Although practicum students may at times be engaged in administrative tasks (because social workers themselves often have these tasks as a part of their responsibilities), the agency should have enough social work activities in which a student can engage that the student is truly spending the majority of his or her time learning about and practicing social work. Only in this way can students develop the expected competencies of generalist or advanced social work practice.

Another important consideration for social work students seeking practicum placements is the nature of the organizational setting: Is the organization predominantly staffed by social workers, with the major practice methods and value base informed by the social work profession, or is the organization a "host setting," where the social worker may be the only social work professional in the agency, working in a transdisciplinary way with other providers and practitioners? Both types of practicum settings can provide valuable experience to students, but it is important for students to have information about the nature of specific organizational settings (Royse, Dhopper, & Rompf, 2012).

In some communities, there is a shortage of social workers with degrees from accredited programs and/or state licensure. This is especially true in many rural communities. Degreed and licensed social workers can sometimes take on the role of social work field instructor at an agency where they are not formally employed. This enables some agencies that provide services in rural areas or that use innovative practice approaches to take on students despite not having a social worker on staff. In this case, the student would have a "task supervisor" at the agency, someone to oversee the student's daily activities, while meeting with the licensed social worker for supervision at least twice a month. Having the outside social work supervision enables students to gain a clearer understanding of the professional identity of social work as well as the knowledge base and competencies expected of social workers.

> **Case Example:** Robin was a BSW student at a university in a predominantly rural area of the state. Robin wanted to have her junior-year practicum at The Empowerment Center, a drop-in center in the town, because this agency offered some innovative programming for adults with serious mental illness. However, the agency had only one social worker on staff, and that social worker did not have the time to provide weekly field education supervision. Rather than reject the possibility of a practicum placement at The Empowerment Center, the social worker was able to recruit another staff member who had a master's degree in counseling psychology to serve as "task supervisor" for Robin. Robin worked closely with the task supervisor to learn practice methods and techniques. She met on alternate weeks with the social worker (her field instructor of record) and with her task supervisor. Robin felt good about this arrangement, as she was able to discuss issues related specifically to the social work professional identity, while also receiving ongoing mentoring and support in her work.

LEARNING ABOUT THE FIELD INSTRUCTOR ROLE

College and university social work programs provide regular orientations to their field education programs. For example, at Augsburg

College, where I teach, we offer a "Field Instructor Welcome" to our affiliated field instructors in August, before the start of the academic year. This "Welcome" event provides an opportunity for us to ensure that our field instructors understand the policies and procedures of our field education program, and it also provides an excellent networking opportunity and chance for us to meet field instructors face to face before our students start their practicum hours. We devote some time to smaller break-out sessions as well, where field instructors can bring their questions and talk with other professionals about effective social work supervision. The break-out sessions offer opportunities to go into more detail about school policies and Council on Social Work Education (CSWE) expectations. They help field instructors to become familiar with our college's assessment forms and expectations for students' learning.

It is important to attend these "Welcome" and "Orientation" events. Through these training opportunities, you can gain greater familiarity with the roles and expectations of specific schools' departments and programs. Meeting field seminar faculty as well as field education directors can also help you link a name with a face if you need help or have questions during the course of working with your practicum student. These field orientations can also be helpful in introducing you to current theory and practice methods related to field education. This knowledge can help you to fine-tune your supervisory style to best meet the needs of incoming students (Weiss et al., 2008).

If questions arise when your student is beginning his or her work with you, know that field seminar faculty and field education directors are eager to help you foster your student's success. You should always feel welcome to contact faculty or administrative staff at the social work program if concerns appear.

Chapter 2 of this book provides an introduction to the roles and responsibilities of field instructors, with much useful advice on how to engage in successful field education with social work students.

WHAT ARE REASONABLE EXPECTATIONS OF A
SOCIAL WORK PRACTICUM STUDENT?

Dezette Johnson, in a 2011 article in *Field Educator*, enumerated a basic list of skills and behaviors that are expected of professional social workers. They are as follows:

- Oral communication
- Written communication
- Beginning generalist social work skills (including application of classroom knowledge to practice, assessment and treatment planning skills, and respect for diversity)
- Professionalism
- Workplace skills (such as appropriate dress and adaptability to the office routine)
(Johnson, 2011)

These basics should all be incorporated into the expectations and learning agendas of students. Students with little workplace experience may need more introduction and explanation of these basic skills. Older students who have substantial work histories are likely to have a better grasp of skills such as professionalism and appropriate workplace behaviors (Everett, Miehls, DuBois, & Garran, 2011).

An important area to cover at the beginning of the practicum is agency-specific information that the student will need to perform well. Students need to be oriented to the agency and its history, mission, values, and programming. Students need information pertaining to agency policies on such topics as safety, use of restraints, professional ethics, and use of evidence-based interventions. Having students attend an orientation session with other volunteers or incoming staff can be helpful. However, it is also important to orient the student to the specific role played by interns in the particular agency setting.

Expectations need to be clear. A practicum student is not a cheap replacement for a paid staff position. Students should have the opportunity to work with clients and develop certain practice skills, but this opportunity should be situated in appropriate training and mentoring, as well as the chance to shadow experienced practitioners before conducting a practice activity alone (Danowski, 2012). The CSWE Educational Policies and Accreditation Standards (EPAS) provide guidance on developing specific tasks and activities to promote acquisition of expected skills (CSWE, 2008). It is helpful to work collaboratively with the student to develop a learning assessment that will serve as a guide to the learning process (see Chapter 4).

Students have the right to adequate supervision in the practicum setting—at least 1 hour of protected time for supervision each week (Royse, Dhopper, & Rompf, 2012). Even if field instructor and student are working side by side for much of the practicum student's time, the student still needs face-to-face time to discuss and process internship activities. Development of a strong, honest relationship with the social work field instructor has been recognized as one of students' most important determinants of a positive practicum experience, and protected time for supervision contributes to that strong relationship (Ornstein & Moses, 2010).

Students should adhere to agency expectations regarding dress, language, and boundaries (Johnson, 2011). The field instructor should clearly communicate these expectations, as some agencies have a much more informal practice climate than others. Once students are aware of the agency culture, they should be held accountable for meeting those expectations (Danowski, 2012).

Students should understand that neither agency staff nor agency clientele are their friends (Reamer, 2012). This is discussed in more detail in Chapter 9 of this volume. Students should be educated about the appropriate level of professionalism. Students will want to have pleasant, collaborative relationships with staff and clients, but they also need to respect healthy professional boundaries, and especially to be clear in initial contacts with clients about what those boundaries mean.

LEGAL AND PRACTICAL CONSIDERATIONS

Liability/Malpractice Insurance

Most social work programs will require students entering field placements to obtain their own liability insurance. Although lawsuits against social work practicum students and their agency hosts may be rare, it is important for students as a matter of professional preparation to be covered for this possibility (Royse et al., 2012). In many cases, students can obtain low-cost insurance by joining their state's chapter of the NASW.

Work Space

Students should be provided with a desk, cubicle, or other work area (Royse et al., 2012). If students will be doing a great deal of writing or data entry into an electronic records system, they should be provided with a desktop or laptop computer that they can use for these tasks. The field instructor should inform the student of a conference room or other space that is available for meetings with clients, families, or client groups.

Supervisory Availability

Before taking on a practicum student, you will need to feel confident that you have the time in your schedule to provide supervision as well as appropriate mentorship to the student. You will need to be able to set aside 1 hour per week to meet face to face with the student to discuss the student's progress in meeting learning goals (Lotmore, 2014). In addition, students may need further training or mentorship as they learn discrete practice skills and gain more confidence in working with agency clients or programs (Harris, 2011).

GETTING READY

Just as the start of a new practicum can be both an exciting and anxiety-provoking experience for the social work student, the beginning of a practicum can create anxiety for the field instructor as well (Lotmore, 2014). Take the time to prepare for the internship; this could involve ensuring that you are familiar with the college/university policies or reading some inspiring material on social work supervision. Lotmore (2014) describes her own process of familiarizing herself with field instruction by reading professional literature on the topic. Chapter 3 of this book will provide more information on how to start the practicum on a positive note.

CONCLUSION

The social work practicum is an indispensable aspect of social work education (Danowski, 2012). Although much important learning happens in the social work classroom, it is essential that students have the opportunity to take their knowledge into a real-world agency setting, so that they can learn what "real-life" social workers do, and how their classroom experiences have helped to prepare them for the serious work of helping other people (Wayne, Bogo, & Raskin, 2010). Whether you are working in health care, child protection, mental health services, corrections, education, gerontology, or another area of social work practice, you have much important knowledge to share with a student. You have an incredible opportunity to mentor a future social worker. Your education and practice wisdom can help a current student to become a knowledgeable, skilled, and ethical professional. This is an amazing opportunity, as well as a grave responsibility.

I have been fortunate to have some outstanding BSW and MSW practicum students over the years. Sharing my work with them has been a great pleasure. It is also rewarding to watch students grow in their maturity and their level of professional skill. As with the rest of our professional activities as social workers, becoming an effective field instructor requires knowledge and practice. Use the resources available at your agency and at colleges or universities in your area to enhance your understanding of effective supervision and field instruction.

REFERENCES

Birkenmaier, J. (2011). Promoting social justice within the practicum. In L. M. Grobman (Ed.), *The field placement survival guide: What you need to know to get the most from your social work practicum* (2nd ed., pp. 241–248). Harrisburg, PA: White Hat Communications.

Council on Social Work Education. (2008). *Educational policy and accreditation standards.* Alexandria, VA: Author.

Danowski, W. A. (2012). *In the field: A guide for the social work practicum* (2nd ed.). Boston, MA: Pearson Education.

Everett, J. E., Miehls, D., DuBois, C., & Garran, A. M. (2011). The developmental model of supervision as reflected in the experiences of field supervisors and graduate students. *Journal of Teaching in Social Work, 31*(3), 250–264.

Harris, E. G. (2011). The reflecting team in supervision of social work interns. *Field Educator, 1*(1). Retrieved June 4, 2015, from http://fieldeducator.simmons.edu/article/the-reflecting-team-in-supervision-of-social-work-interns/

Johnson, D. (2011, October). Readiness for field: What do field instructors think? *Field Educator, 1*(1). Retrieved June 4, 2015, from http://fieldeducator.simmons.edu/article/readiness-for-field-what-do-field-instructors-think/

Lotmore, A. (2014). Whos, whats, and hows of being a successful social work field supervisor. *The New Social Worker, 21*(1), 6–7.

Ornstein, E. D., & Moses, H. (2010). Goodness of fit: A relational approach to field instruction. *Journal of Teaching in Social Work, 30*(1), 101–114.

Reamer, F. (2012). Essential ethics education in social work field education. *Field Educator, 2*(2). Retrieved March 14, 2015, from http://www.fieldeducator.simmons.edu/article/essential-ethics-education-in-social-work-field-instruction/

Royse, D., Dhopper, S. S., & Rompf, E. L. (2012). *Field instruction: A guide for social work students* (Updated ed.). Boston, MA: Pearson Education.

Ward, K., & Mama, R. S. (2010). *Breaking out of the box: Adventure-based field instruction* (2nd ed.). Chicago, IL: Lyceum.

Wayne, J., Bogo, M., & Raskin, M. (2010, Fall). Field education as the signature pedagogy of social work education. *Journal of Social Work Education, 46*(3), 327–339.

Weiss, I., Gal, J., & Cnaan, R. A. (2008). Social work education as professional socialization. *Journal of Social Service Research, 31*(1), 13–31.

TWO

Facilitating Positive School–Field Agency Collaboration

Melissa A. Hensley

When social work practitioners agree to take on interns from a social work degree program, they are agreeing to work hand in hand with the students to ensure that the students meet the learning requirements, often expressed as competencies, of the social work program (Council on Social Work Education [CSWE], 2008). Because the field experience is the primary setting in which students are able to apply their academic learning to professional practice, successful completion of the social work practica is necessary for students to advance in their degree requirements and to graduate. An important element of ensuring a good experience for the practicum student is to engage actively with the student's social work school or department. There are "built-in" expectations around communication and site visits for the practicum experience, but field instructors should feel welcome to be in contact with the school throughout the student's internship experience. Field education coordinators, as well as field seminar faculty, can be a wonderful source of information and resources, and can also help in ensuring the most helpful experience possible for each practicum student.

THE DEVELOPMENT OF SCHOOL–FIELD AGENCY COLLABORATION: BACKGROUND

Effective communication between the academic institution and the field instructor/agency setting is indispensable to the social work practicum process. It is important for the school or program to understand the characteristics of agencies offering social work practicum positions, as well as the potential learning opportunities that each agency provides (Tully, 2015). Smooth communication is also key when a student is in the midst of a practicum placement, to ensure that field instructors are aware of trainings/orientations, paperwork requirements and deadlines, and expected learning outcomes for students from a particular program.

WHO'S WHO IN THE SOCIAL WORK PROGRAM?

Each college and university social work school or program operates somewhat differently, but the following job titles and roles are frequently found in the field education programs of social work schools and departments.

Field Education Coordinator or Director

This individual is a member of the department who coordinates practicum placements for students in a particular program. Social work departments that offer more than one degree program may have a separate field education coordinator for bachelor's degree in social work (BSW) and master's degree in social work (MSW) programs. The field education coordinator is a great source of knowledge about the policies and procedures of the department and helps to match interested students with appropriate practicum agencies. Some field education coordinators are considered administrative staff within their department and may or may not have teaching or other academic responsibilities. At other social work schools or programs, the field education coordinator is a full-time faculty member with field education administrative responsibilities. In either instance, the person in this position will possess in-depth knowledge of the practicum process.

Field Education Seminar Faculty

The field education seminar instructor (also sometimes referred to as the "faculty field liaison") coordinates and teaches the seminar course that many social work students enroll in while they are completing their fieldwork (Ward & Mama, 2010). Field seminar faculty may be full-time faculty in the social work program, or they may be adjunct or part-time instructors. The seminar provides a place for students to review and process in depth the skills they are learning in the practicum. In many programs, the field seminar faculty member is the person who conducts site visits at the students' practicum settings and is the first contact if a student is experiencing problems. In sum, field education seminar faculty members are responsible for "bridging the relationships between the program, the field instructor, and the internship student" (Tully, 2015, p. 6).

Faculty Advisor

Every student in a social work degree program should have an academic advisor. This faculty member helps students plan their course scheduling and serves as a mentor for students as they consider their career goals. The extent of the advisor's involvement in the student's academic career varies from one program to the next. In some programs, the student may be required to meet with his or her advisor a prescribed number of times during the academic year, whereas in other programs, no formal contact with the academic advisor is required. In some social work programs, faculty advisors conduct site visits for their students' practicum placements. It is helpful for field instructors to know the faculty member serving as the practicum student's advisor because the advisor can offer a listening ear and be an advocate for the student.

HOW DO YOU ENSURE GOOD COMMUNICATION BETWEEN THE COLLEGE AND THE FIELD AGENCY?

As mentioned in Chapter 1, social work programs usually offer a welcome session or orientation for field instructors prior to students' starting their practicum work. It is especially important to attend these sessions if you are just beginning a collaboration with a particular college or university's field education program. Although many practicum policies and guidelines are dictated by accreditation standards from the CSWE, each department or program handles field education somewhat differently, and attending welcome/orientation sessions can clarify the practices of a specific program. These sessions also provide an opportunity to "connect names with faces" among the full-time faculty who serve as field liaisons or seminar leaders, as well as to network with other agencies hosting practicum students. Many field orientation sessions will also include time for field instructors to bring up questions or concerns, which can then be addressed by the field education coordinator or other personnel from the school.

Regular electronic communication can be helpful, especially regarding policies that are important for agencies and the college/university to observe (Royse, Dhopper, & Rompf, 2012). For example, are there policies related to safety that all students should follow? How do these policies connect with the safety policies set forth by the agency? Social work programs or schools may also maintain a website for field education materials, where field instructors and students can go to find templates of necessary forms as well as field education policy manuals.

Staying connected to the social work school's web presence is particularly important. Different schools and programs handle social media, blogs, and web pages differently, and it is helpful to familiarize yourself with the school or program's web page. Increasingly, field education web pages are being used as a repository for learning assessment templates, handbooks and policy documents, as well as basic guidelines for the field education program. The University of Pittsburgh, for example, has an attractive, well-organized website for field education in its social work programs (University of Pittsburgh School of Social Work, n.d.).

Communicating with the college or university when students are experiencing problems is also important. This is discussed in more detail in Chapter 7. Communication with the faculty field liaison and/or the field education director is critical when students are having problems. When school administrators and faculty find out about problems early on, there is a greater chance that the issue can be resolved and that the field instructor and student will both have a positive overall experience (Ward & Mama, 2010).

COLLABORATION: ENSURING INTEGRATION OF CLASSROOM AND FIELD SETTING

One of the biggest responsibilities in the implementation of "signature pedagogy" is ensuring that practicum students can successfully integrate the knowledge they gain in the classroom with the real-world practice of social work. This work of integration happens in a variety of ways: through learning and practicing effective social work methods, exploring the impact of social policy on agency clients, and applying a theoretical perspective to a client or agency situation in order to better select an intervention approach (see Chapter 6, for example). Integrating classroom content with practicum experience is much easier when students talk to field instructors about the things they are learning in class (Royse et al., 2012). One way to keep abreast of students' learning is to have access to syllabi for each practicum student's courses. This is much easier now that almost all course syllabi are available to students in electronic form. Field instructors should encourage students to share syllabi with them. As field instructors strive to integrate classroom knowledge and theory with practicum activities, knowing what students are reading and discussing is extremely helpful.

Case Example: Marianne was a school social worker who had served as a field instructor for many years. Marianne had accepted Thomas, a senior-year BSW student from a nearby social work school at a well-respected university, as her intern for that academic year. Because of her years of experience, Marianne felt that she had a reasonable understanding of the competencies expected of BSW students. She found herself wishing that she had more contact with the staff and faculty of Thomas's social work program, however. Although Thomas demonstrated professionalism and established rapport with students fairly quickly, he was reluctant to discuss the content of his courses in supervisory meetings with Marianne. When Thomas's field seminar faculty member came for the midterm visit, Marianne mentioned her desire to more explicitly connect course content with Thomas's activities in the practicum. The field seminar faculty encouraged Thomas to share his course syllabi with Marianne and explained to Thomas the importance of being able to apply knowledge and concepts from class to the work of the internship. In addition, the field seminar faculty was able to ensure that Marianne was on the university's e-mail mailing list so that she would receive information about upcoming continuing education and networking events sponsored by the school. Marianne felt that this contact with the school helped her do her job as a field instructor with more confidence.

Positive communication with faculty members who teach field education seminars is also valuable for field instructors. Field faculty should be educating themselves about the agencies at which students are doing their practica (Tully, 2015). One way that field faculty accomplish that is by having students give formal presentations on their agencies during the field seminar. This helps students to acquire more in-depth knowledge about their practicum agencies, and it educates the field faculty member as well as the other students about the activities and programs at that student's practicum site. If a student comes to supervision asking for detailed information about the organization and its activities as a whole, field instructors should provide such information or direct students to a source for that knowledge. Some examples of resources that are helpful for student learning are provided in Chapter 3. In addition, field instructors should share any web-based information resources related to the agency; many social service and health care organizations have their history, mission, and values posted on their websites. Sharing web addresses and other sources of agency information can help you foster a collaborative relationship with field faculty as well as your practicum student.

If a practicum student is struggling or not meeting agency expectations for interns' performance, the field instructor should contact the field faculty and/or the field education coordinator sooner rather than later. When students' challenges can be addressed earlier, there is a better chance that the student, school, and agency can develop a plan for performance improvement (see Chapters 7 and 9). There are many times when students may be struggling early in the semester, but with guidance and mentoring from the field instructor and seminar faculty, the student can better meet the learning expectations of the program.

Site visits can play an important role in positive school–agency relationships. Most social work programs require three contacts between field faculty and the field instructor over the course of a student's practicum, and at least two of these should consist of in-person visits (Royse et al., 2012). These visits help the field instructor to feel a stronger connection to the school, and they help provide "a face to go with the name" in case further communication is needed. Usually, these visits are fairly routine, with a discussion of the student's tasks and performance and perhaps a brief tour of the agency. Field faculty or field liaisons may ask questions pertaining to specific practice methods or skills being learned, discussion of ethics at the practicum agency, and/or students' understanding of theoretical frameworks that guide practice at the agency. If the student is encountering problems in his or her performance, then this should definitely be discussed at the in-person site visits or during telephone conferences. Following up on communication related to the student's performance during the site visit can help ensure that the student remains "on track."

> **Case Example:** Greg was a social worker who was employed as a development director at Holistic Services, a large local nonprofit social service agency. He had accepted Thea, a macro-practice-concentration social work student, to work with him on tasks related to grant writing and the agency's annual fundraising campaign. This was Greg's first time as a field instructor. Because Greg was not an experienced field instructor, he made an extra effort to attend training events at Thea's college, and he stayed in communication with the field seminar faculty member as he and Thea developed her learning agenda. Greg and Thea were able to establish a productive relationship as Thea completed a variety of tasks and activities related to development and fundraising. Toward the end of the fall semester, Thea's field seminar faculty came to Holistic Services to meet with Greg and Thea. Greg was able to use this opportunity to clarify expectations about student evaluation and brainstorm with the faculty member about ways to include content about ethics and other topics related to professional identity into Thea's practicum experience.

Field instructors should also take advantage of opportunities to visit social work departments and connect with faculty and students on campus. Social work programs vary greatly in the opportunities they offer for affiliated field instructors, but many offer networking events or free/reduced-price continuing education programming for their field instructors. These can help field instructors feel more connected to the school, and they can also be a good source of ongoing training in effective supervision.

CONCLUSION

Maintaining steady lines of communication between field agencies and colleges/universities is a major responsibility that is shared by field instructors, field seminar faculty, and field education directors. Site visits serve as a structure for school–agency communication. They are important in ensuring that students are acquiring necessary skills and that field instructors are meeting the school's expectations for training and supervision. Fostering strong communication between agencies and colleges/universities may also involve electronic, phone, or in-person communication over the course of a student's practicum experience. Field instructors should always feel comfortable contacting a liaison at a school if questions arise or problems with a student's performance occur.

REFERENCES

Council on Social Work Education. (2008). *Educational policy and accreditation standards.* Alexandria, VA: Author.

Royse, D., Dhopper, S. S., & Rompf, E. L. (2012). *Field instruction: A guide for social work students* (Updated ed.). Boston, MA: Pearson Education.

Tully, G. (2015). The faculty field liaison: An essential role for advancing graduate and undergraduate group work education. *Social Work with Groups, 38,* 6–20.

University of Pittsburgh School of Social Work. (n.d.). *Field education.* Retrieved June 10, 2015, from http://www.socialwork.pitt.edu/academics/field-education

THREE

A Checklist of Dos and Don'ts

Mary Simonson Clark

The purpose of this chapter is to provide an overview of ways in which you can work to ensure a positive experience for you and your social work practicum student. Written by a social worker with extensive experience as a field instructor in several community-based organizations, this chapter offers some helpful, practical advice to guide the field instructor–student relationship. Presented in a checklist of "dos and don'ts," the chapter provides a great deal of practice-based wisdom for the field instructor.

AS YOU BEGIN . . .

Don't make the assumption that the new intern is the same person as your last intern or that the experience will be identical. If this is your first intern, **don't** assume that the intern will approach the internship as you approached your internship. **Do** keep in mind the social work value of the dignity and worth of the individual—it applies to students as well as clients! **Do** be ready for the excitement and challenges of a unique experience.

DO COMMENCE THOROUGHLY: INITIAL CONVERSATIONS

Don't assume all the information you need about the intern is on the application form. **Don't** ask the intern to "hit the ground running" without taking the time to have some thorough conversations about the experience and expectations—both yours and those of the intern. Commencing with thorough, transparent, clear, and specific conversations can minimize future misunderstandings and maximize the intern's growth in what the intern is more likely to perceive as a safe learning environment.

Do spend ample time initially getting to know your intern. Share enough of yourself that the intern will be comfortable with you and understand the boundaries of your relationship. If your intern is willing to share, it will be useful to gather some information that will help determine the hours the individual can commit to an internship and the additional responsibilities the intern may face in his or her daily life. Information-gathering questions that may be useful for you to ask the intern include the following:

- Are you a full- or part-time student?
- Are you a student athlete or member of a music group (e.g., band, orchestra, choir, etc.), or do you have other commitments that affect your availability?
- What is your class schedule this term? Will it change in future terms?
- Do you have a full- or part-time job?
- Do you have caregiver responsibilities you must accommodate in your schedule?
- Do you participate in any group meetings (e.g., social, faith, support, etc.) that you do not want to miss or cannot forego?
- Are there days and/or times that you cannot participate in the internship and/or supervision? (This may relate to religious practices.)

- How many hours per week do you plan to commit to the internship?
- Which days and times are you available?
- By what approximate time (i.e., month and week) do you hope to finish your internship?

Many students choose to or must meet enormous responsibilities, and they balance complex schedules. Knowing about these circumstances from the beginning of the internship (and preferably even before making a commitment to the internship) can dramatically decrease conflicts, stress, and unmet goals. It is also important for you to be clear about the organization's needs in terms of hours, days, and the duration of the internship. Establishing open lines of communication so students will be proactive in seeking your input, guidance, or permission to meet changes and challenges can decrease anxiety, which will help ensure their maximum learning, growth, and performance in the practicum.

> **Case Example: Inadequate Initial Relationship Building:** The field instructor looked forward to supervising an intern close to her own age who was working in older-adult care. In this policy internship, the instructor was an itinerant field instructor with a nonlicensed on-site task supervisor who holds a master's degree in social work (MSW). The instructor had policy and macro-practice experience, previously worked in long-term care, and was her parents' caregiver. This appeared to be a good supervisor–intern fit. The intern had a specific idea for her summative project, which the task supervisor agreed would be informative for his policy work.
>
> However, the intern had decided what would be the appropriate findings before beginning the work. Together they began developing the learning agenda, but the work did not progress well. It became increasingly difficult to schedule supervision. The supervisor learned that in addition to academics and the internship, the intern was working a full-time job in older-adult

care and had a part-time job in a group home. She was determined to keep her schedule of daily responsibilities, social events, vacations, and so forth as a partner, mother, and friend. A death in the instructor's family and of the intern's beloved family pet further strained the internship.

By midterm, the intern was dissatisfied with her internship site. The field faculty, with agreement of the task supervisor and field instructor, added a site linked to the research, but reminded the intern that her primary responsibility was to her initial placement. The intern did not follow through with recommendations and relied heavily on the supervisor to lead her through her written work. She was irritated when research contacts did not respond, did not follow up with further communication, allowed inadequate time for the work, and failed to have a realistic perspective on research or an alternative plan.

The intern failed to provide research findings for the task supervisor's policy work. Her senior academic year ended without completion of some of her internship goals and her summative project. She filed for an extension and took another full year to complete her work. She was displeased with the instructor's final evaluation that she had not acted professionally, shown respect for other people's schedules, or fulfilled her responsibilities in a timely manner. It also was a learning experience for the field instructor, who recognized that she must spend more time initially in getting to know interns and their complex schedules, establishing solid relationships, building good communication, and developing clear expectations about supervision, responsibilities, professional behavior, respect of colleagues, and timely completion of assignments.

Don't assume all interns communicate the way you communicate or access the communication methods your staff and organization use. Not only has information technology changed personal communication, it has dramatically changed communication within academic institutions. Both you and the intern may need to compromise and learn some new as well as different methods of communication. Understanding communication methods and styles is particularly critical in working with students who have disabilities, to make sure that students are able to communicate effectively with you, other staff, and agency clients/stakeholders.

Do have a clear discussion about communication expectations and styles. Be specific. Find out the best way to communicate with the intern, particularly if you need to reach the intern on short notice. Useful questions about communication may include the following:

- What is the best way to contact you (e.g., a phone call, e-mail, or text message)?
- What is your preferred phone number and e-mail address?
- May I leave voice mails? Should I leave messages with a certain person?

Do also be clear about how the intern can and should communicate with you. Consider clearly sharing the following information with the intern:

- The way(s) the intern can reach you most effectively
- How and when the intern should communicate with you in cases of illness or emergency
- How promptly you expect the intern to respond to your communication (e.g. within hours, within the day, within 2 days, etc.)
- How promptly the intern can expect you to respond

Don't allow students to cross boundaries of personal time with internship time. **Do** be clear about the intern's personal use of a cell phone during internship hours, including supervision. Explain the limitations regarding use of the organization's phone, e-mail, and Internet for personal use and work-related use. Be specific about what is and is not acceptable by framing it in the context of social work professional behavior. Role model that same behavior!

Don't expect or encourage students to use their personal phone or e-mail account with clients or other agencies. This is a matter of consideration in terms of students' costs, safety, professionalism, and confidentiality, which extends to confidentiality with clients and agencies. **Do** make sure the intern has use of the organization's phone and e-mail system.

Don't assume the intern understands confidentiality. In a time of prevalent social media, the lines of confidentiality are often blurred and the consequences are frequently devastating. **Do** be very clear about what interns may share and with whom. **Do** review step by step how your organization maintains confidentiality for clients and with collaborative partners. Encourage interns to come to you immediately with any questions as well as if they feel they may have violated confidentiality policies. Although it is difficult and complex, learning the intricacies of confidentiality is essential. This may include familiarizing the practicum student with relevant laws and policies that may affect your setting—for example, the Health Insurance Portability and Accountability Act in inpatient and outpatient health care settings (Ligon & Ward, 2011).

Don't assume that interns learn in the same manner as you learn. **Don't** presume they have no special needs just because they do not exhibit apparent disabilities. **Do** ask interns how they best learn, as well as what they perceive they will need and expect from you. It may be helpful to discuss various mentoring and supervisory options with interns. In particular, students without relevant work experience may benefit from an explanation of the professional supervision process.

Do ask if interns require any accommodations and convey that you are willing to work with them and, if needed, with staff at the school's disability services office, so that they can successfully participate in the organization's work and achieve their personal optimal potential.

Don't let interns feel they are not welcome, valued, or part of your organization. Also, **don't** let clients and colleagues question the identity of interns. **Do** make sure interns have name tags or badges similar to those of staff members. These name tags should clearly indicate that they are interns, and you should introduce your students as interns.

Case Example: Supervising Across Cultures: The field instructor was supervising an intern from a culture unfamiliar to her. During their initial meeting, the intern was resolute to share the story about her brother, who had died in a violent conflict, and her family's perspective, which was not covered by media. The supervisor deviated from the initial orientation, allowed time for sharing, and offered empathetic responses.

After the initial orientation, as the instructor and intern worked together on the learning agreement, the instructor struggled with how she should approach the intern's inadequate writing skills. Building on the open communication established initially, the intern explained that her difficulty with writing in English, her second language, was a challenge shared by other students from her culture. The instructor paused to learn more about the intern's language and the very advanced academic degrees earned by her siblings. Recognizing that academic success was a value for the intern, the instructor proceeded to provide more writing support and outside resources. It was apparent that improving writing skills was a necessary part of the intern's learning to complete professional reports.

During the internship, a globally renowned leader in the intern's culture, who had a close relationship with the intern's family, passed away. The intern's family and community were in deep mourning. Again, the open communication established initially provided a safe space for the intern to explain this grieving process, share the losses her family experienced in their emigration, and describe the pain her community felt because past contributions to the United States were not recognized.

Cross-cultural challenges continued. The internship concluded with the student struggling to balance responsibilities of employment, academics, and family cultural roles of wife, mother, and daughter. Based on the cultural learning and relationship the instructor and intern had established, they discussed ways the intern might deal with these competing responsibilities. They successfully completed the internship, both having served as instructors and learners based on the open communication, awareness, and trust established during the initial supervision.

Don't assume that the intern understands the organization's context and the safety precautions that may be critical. **Do** explain clearly where the intern should park or what transportation is a safe, accessible option. Discuss safety in coming and going from the site. Cover the use of keys and locking doors, equipment, and supplies. In addition, make sure the student knows how to get assistance from other staff members or from outside emergency personnel. **Do** give the intern a careful tour of the facilities, including the locations of:

- Fire extinguishers
- First aid kits, including automated external defibrillators (AEDs)
- Storm shelters
- Exits
- Security systems

Due to the critical importance of safety, **do** consider reviewing safety procedures once the intern has been at the site for a few weeks. Determine the level of first aid training the intern may have had previously; if it is inadequate for your practice, ensure that the intern receives additional training. Discuss options that may be available in the community for cardiopulmonary resuscitation (CPR) and first aid training. Review safety procedures when it appears situations may warrant quick action (e.g., impending storms, clients who might act out, medical conditions requiring rapid intervention, etc.). **Do** review safety procedures during supervision meetings.

Do ensure that students have access to any available policies or manuals that are used by agency staff or volunteers.

It is essential to be thorough as the practicum begins. Your actions in these initial conversations, including getting to know the intern, sharing some of yourself without crossing boundaries, establishing lines of communication, clarifying expectations, attending to details, and conveying critical information, comprise potent role modeling for students. Your efforts at effective communication and authentic relationship building help students to understand the level of effort they need to put into relationships with their clients, colleagues, and collaborative organizations. However, initial conversations, including the enormous amount of information you need to convey, require continuous, intentional follow-up throughout the internship, particularly within your ongoing supervision with the student.

Do help interns make use of the following resources as they get acquainted with the organization and its stakeholders:

- Mission statement
- Agency strategic plan
- Annual reports
- Agency policy and procedure manuals
- Agency website
- Websites of agencies giving or receiving referrals

DO CONTINUE INTENTIONALLY: ONGOING SUPERVISION

Don't think of supervision as something that will occur naturally. Professional social work supervision is critical to the development of professional identity and to the acquisition of practice skills. **Don't** begin the practicum experience by letting students think that supervision is optional. **Don't** get in the habit of frequently canceling or postponing intentional supervisory meetings. Scheduled supervision should be protected time devoted to the professional development of the practicum student.

Do let interns know from the start that supervision is an integral part of their learning experience. Ensure they understand that it is their right to expect and require supervision for 1 hour each week. In addition, make sure they understand that this is a professional internship requirement, mandated by the Council on Social Work Education (CSWE), that you will be intentional in fulfilling (CSWE, 2008). **Do**

remind interns that supervision is also a time that you, and therefore the organization, can learn from their experiences and insights.

Some interns and supervisors do well in waiting to schedule supervision each week depending on the contextual circumstances. However, this can easily result in delaying supervision when schedules become busy—and schedules are frequently busy. It may be best to set up a specific time and day each week to meet with the student for supervision. It may be helpful for you to provide specific criteria regarding when it is and is not acceptable to cancel or delay supervision.

Supervision is intentional; **don't** dismiss it as conversations done in passing or while walking together between meetings.

You can provide supervision individually with the student or, if two or more students are at a placement site, in a group. Group supervision should only account for half of the total supervision hours. Group supervision allows students to learn from each other and problem solve together. However, as a supervisor, it is important to ensure that all interns contribute to the process. Group supervision cannot replace confidential, one-on-one supervision, which must occur for half of the total supervisory hours. Treat each student as an individual who will have unique questions, concerns, learning style, and growth.

Don't make supervision solely your responsibility as the supervisor. **Do** help interns own the practicum and take responsibility for their learning during supervision. You and the interns can do this with the use of an agenda. The process of learning how to develop an agenda has many benefits, which include the following:

- Ensuring that interns receive answers to their questions of which you may be unaware
- Helping interns review their progress, organize their thoughts, and prepare for supervision
- Using supervision time efficiently and as scheduled
- Developing the skill of preparing for and leading a meeting within an organization or the community
- Planning and timing presentations

Learning to develop an agenda is a process. **Do** begin by asking interns simply to suggest one or two items as a focus for supervision. **Do** communicate to interns that you will offer agenda items that you determine are important for their learning and growth or relate to their circumstances. Encourage interns to progress toward a full, timed agenda that they share a day or more in advance of supervision. Guide students to appreciate that this professional behavior helps you, as well as colleagues attending a meeting, come well prepared for an efficient, productive meeting. **Don't** surprise students with topics during supervision; **do** try to consistently provide your agenda items in advance of supervision. If interns wish to discuss an article, assignment, research, or other information, encourage them to provide you with the materials well in advance of the supervision; you may wish to set a specific time frame for this.

Providing you with advance notice is also critical if interns require your input for any of their academic assignments. **Do** remind interns that although they are very busy, staff members are also busy. Discuss that professionalism and respect improve collegial relationships. Role model this respect with interns and colleagues. Directly, clearly, and consistently express appreciation when interns and colleagues respectfully consider your time and schedule.

Don't forget the intern's learning agenda and assessment or agreement. **Do** encourage the intern to use this as a guide for developing the supervision agenda. Suggest that the intern make careful notes about how he or she has accomplished objectives and add these to the supervision agenda. By intentionally working through the objectives in supervision, midterm and final evaluations become affirming summaries and reviews rather than stressful discussions of unmet expectations or unaddressed concerns.

Case Example: Brainstorming Contextual Challenges: The field instructor was supervising a graduate intern in a large funding agency with an on-site task supervisor. Soon, the very capable, conscientious, and self-reflective intern expressed concerns the task supervisor did not respond to her learning needs.

Cautious about undermining the task supervisor's authority, the instructor encouraged the intern to speak directly with the supervisor. There was no perceptible change in responsiveness. Having established good communication in off-site supervision, the instructor and intern brainstormed possible reasons for the responsiveness challenges and problem solved potential approaches to resolve the problems. They considered that personal circumstances and job dissatisfaction can influence professional behavior. Shortly, the task supervisor left the agency for another position he perceived would be more fulfilling.

Inadequate responsiveness was not the intern's only concern. Although the agency interacted with organizations serving communities that were marginalized and ethnically diverse, the agency's leaders were almost exclusively from the dominant culture. Again cautious to respect the agency yet help the intern learn, the instructor and intern brainstormed ways agencies can incorporate diversity into decisions. When the intern repeatedly recognized that the agency was not responding to organizations' concerns, the instructor had the intern verbalize other approaches and macro-practice models she could institute as a potential future agency leader.

They also frequently considered dual relationships or conflicts of interest, particularly in funding competition to maintain essential programs. They discussed procedures and decisions that could avoid ethical dilemmas. In their discussions, they remained mindful of the intern's current role and limited authority. She successfully completed her internship and recognized that she did not want employment in a similar macro-practice context.

DO CONCLUDE THOUGHTFULLY: PROBLEM SOLVING

Don't ignore concerns or allow interns to form quick conclusions. **Do** approach problems openly, supportively, and thoughtfully during supervision, or sooner, if needed. Internships are important times of problem solving. Help interns develop professional techniques and tools that will allow them to formulate thoughtful conclusions in their future social work practice. When concerns about knowledge, skills, or ethics arise with a specific practicum student, it is best for the student, for you, and for the student's social work program to respond quickly.

Don't wait to introduce ethical tools. **Do** consult with faculty from the intern's academic program to determine which ethical tools they include in the curricula. Familiarize yourself with those tools. Help the intern apply ethical tools to problem solve situations the intern encounters with clients, organizations, or policies in order to come to thoughtful conclusions regarding decisions or actions (Harrington & Dolgoff, 2008). You might review a number of ethical tools with the intern and encourage the intern to draw conclusions concerning for which contexts and circumstances each tool is most applicable. **Do** consistently include social work's core values in discussions about making practice conclusions. A useful way to reinforce the core values is to ask the intern to make comparisons and contrasts between the *Code of Ethics* (2008) of the National Association of Social Workers (NASW) and the *Statement of Ethical Principles* (2012) of the International Federation of Social Workers (IFSW). Thereafter, encourage the intern to draw thoughtful conclusions about the similarities and differences as a way of introducing cultural differences and diverse contexts.

Don't fail to address cross-cultural diversity in its broadest sense. **Do** consistently ask the intern to identify the numerous aspects of diversity—ethnicity, gender, socioeconomic status, education, age, sexual orientation, ability, and so forth—reflected in the clients, contextual communities, and partner organizations. **Do** encourage the intern to make thoughtful conclusions about how diversity relates to the challenges that clients, communities, and organizations encounter. Facilitate students' problem solving regarding ways they can address these challenges on micro, mezzo, and macro levels. Work with students to explore and understand the ways in which particular social theories and perspectives inform services to clients—how can various perspectives help social workers understand the causes of social injustice or social problems, and how can these perspectives effectively shape service and advocacy responses? Encourage them to empower clients and communities to self-determine changes and advocate for just solutions.

Don't ignore the relationship between diversity, the ethical value of self-determination, and the identification of potential interventions. **Do** be transparent with interns concerning whether the clients and communities your organization serves are represented among the workers, within the administration, and on the governing bodies. **Don't** be defensive if diversity is underrepresented. **Do** engage with the intern in thoughtful problem solving regarding how diverse voices can be incorporated into the work (e.g., through advisory councils, community surveys, focus groups, etc.). This process of honoring diversity and including multiple perspectives can add meaning to practicum tasks related to research-informed practice as well as cultural responsiveness at the micro, meso, and macro levels. Help the intern come to feasible conclusions that you might seek and/or that the intern can facilitate in future organizations where the intern might serve.

Don't assume that interns think the organization's administration, leadership, policies, and procedures are always correct. No doubt, interns may conclude there are mistakes. Perhaps there are times when interns are correct. **Do** listen to interns without being unprofessional, triangulating, or taking sides. Discuss with interns what evidence they have regarding what they think is wrong or ineffective. Then, ask them to thoughtfully problem solve what might be an effective alternative within the constraints of context, staffing, funding, mission, and other parameters. Remind interns that, at this time, it is not within their authority to make organizational or policy changes. **Do** affirm them for their concern and problem solving. Suggest they keep their insights in mind for a future time when they are in a position to implement change.

> **Case Example: Interns Are Not Staff:** The licensed graduate social worker (LGSW) itinerant field instructor faced challenges of balancing interns' needs and organizations' client work. Ethical dilemmas developed when organizations failed to meet interns'

requirements. Sometimes, interns struggled to meet client needs, perhaps beyond their skills. Frequently, sites misunderstood their internship responsibilities and time commitment. Often sites focused on how interns could serve as unpaid staff, a situation the supervisor had experienced in her training.

The instructor constantly encouraged interns to advocate directly with their task supervisors to meet their learning needs, including an hour of supervision in weeks when they did not meet with the instructor. She explained that they needed to develop advocacy skills to meet future client or community needs. However, the instructor told interns they also could ask field faculty or her to advocate for them; usually interns chose self-advocacy.

In one experience, one graduate and three junior undergraduate interns were at a court-assigned parenting education site. Staff cuts increased pressure on the interns to handle difficult clients. As their internships neared completion, task supervisors asked the interns to continue intermittently without offers of employment or supervision.

The instructor advised the interns to set limits and focus on closure with the site and with clients, who included children already dealing with intermittent relationships with noncustodial parents. She clarified that she would not provide supervision and did not want liability for potential postinternship problems. She asked the interns to discuss with their field faculty the site's request to continue. When the pressure to continue persisted, coupled with difficulties throughout the internship, the instructor notified the interns' academic program and recommended that the setting no longer be offered as an internship site. The program concurred.

Don't forget that interns may have concerns or conflicts with other interns or staff that are more challenging than their concerns with broader organizational issues. **Do** address conflicts promptly by encouraging the intern to speak directly with the person involved.

Encouraging the intern in self-advocacy is a practice that the intern can generalize to clients and communities.

Don't take sides or undermine authority, but **do** mediate, if necessary, and advocate on behalf of the intern if all else fails. As a supervisor, you can facilitate the intern's growth in the ability to consider thoughtfully comments and feedback while concluding whether they are appropriate or applicable. This is both a personal and professional skill. **Do** help the intern consider, in general, that colleagues deal with challenges in their personal contexts, which may influence their professional interactions. **Don't** allow interns to take every comment by clients, interns, or staff members personally. **Do** encourage interns to express empathy with all clients, interns, and staff members. **Do** foster the intern's strength-based perspective that recognizes and values the experiences as well as expertise of all persons.

SUMMARY

Don't fail to see the strengths the student brings to the internship, whether you are at the point of commencing during thorough initial conversations, continuing through intentional and ongoing supervision, or seeking conclusions based on thoughtful problem solving. **Do** approach the intern with empathy and invest your time, energy, and expertise in the student who may someday be your colleague. **Do** be ready for the excitement and challenges of this unique experience.

REFERENCES

Council on Social Work Education. (2008). *Educational policy and accreditation standards.* Alexandria, VA: Author.

Harrington, D., & Dolgoff, R. (2008). Hierarchies of ethical principles for ethical decision-making. *Social Work, Ethics, and Social Welfare*, 2(2), 183–196.

International Federation of Social Workers. (2012). *Statement of ethical principles.* Retrieved June 12, 2015, from http://ifsw.org/policies/statement-of-ethical-principles/

Ligon, J., & Ward, J. (2011). 10 tips for a successful field placement. In L. M. Grobman (Ed.), *The field placement survival guide: What you need to know to get the most from your social work practicum* (2nd ed., pp. 77–79). Harrisburg, PA: White Hat Communications.

National Association of Social Workers. (2008). *Code of ethics of the National Association of Social Workers.* Retrieved March 14, 2015, from http://www.naswdc.org/pubs/code/code.asp

FOUR

Maximizing the Essential Tool: The Learning Agenda

Christina L. Erickson

Student learning in college and university settings has changed over the years as more and more emphasis has been placed on learning competencies and learning outcomes (Fortune, McCarthy, & Abramson, 2001). When many current field instructors received degrees in social work, field placements were not structured by competencies. Some social work programs had "ill-defined, broad, and vague practice dimensions" (Hunter, Moen, & Raskin, 2015, p. 156), and sometimes specific learning was not tied to the field education experience at all. Some programs used contracts to encourage goal-directed learning and clarity among roles (Fox & Zischka, 1989). Not until 2008, when the Council on Social Work Education (CSWE) mandated standards, were field competencies applied to social work education on a national scale. Field instruction has evolved and become more educationally focused since this time, making field placements and the specifics of learning more integrative and, very likely, more effective. With field placements as the heart of the social work educational experience, deemed our signature pedagogy by the CSWE, emphasis on integrating and evaluating learning competencies in the field is essential.

The student *learning agenda,* sometimes called a *learning contract,* is the universal tool that all social work students use to integrate the competencies within their field placement. Competency-based education begins with the end point, identifying the outcomes for student learning and behavior (Hunter et al., 2015). Students identify how the social work competencies are expressed within their agency of practice, and how the student can demonstrate, in concrete ways, the behaviors of a social worker within the field agency. Although the student learning agenda does have contractual characteristics, its main thrust is student learning. In contracts, one could argue that power is balanced among individuals who sign the contract. In field placements, we recognize the small sphere of power students have, as field education is a graded learning experience. Field instructors do have the power to dismiss or fail field students. We suggest using the term *learning agenda,* as it connotes the true process of the field experience: an agenda for learning.

As noted, field placement has been designated the signature pedagogy of social work education by our national academic accrediting body, the CSWE. As a signature pedagogy, the field experience is the "integrative curricular area in which students are socialized to the profession" (Boitel & Fromm, 2014, p. 608). Signature pedagogies also have been identified in other professions, and aim to inculcate "habits of thinking" (Boitel & Fromm, 2014, p. 609). Field instructors are partners with the academic institutions. The integration of course content and guidance from the academic program your students come from provides the structure of the signature pedagogy for the students you work with. Within this designation, schools of social work have flexibility in teaching, learning, and, most important, connecting theory, knowledge, values, and skills with the field practice setting.

A learning agenda supports student learning in several ways. It provides a road map for the field learning experience and clarifies the expectations for the student and the agency, and it also promotes learning through the following methods (Boitel & Fromm, 2014, p. 614):

- Presents new information in a variety of contexts
- Supports active application of the new learning in practice
- Structures supervisory sessions so that discussion of new concepts is framed in light of prior learning
- Allows the student to recognize in the field setting how the new learning benefits clients
- Instills in students the habit of thinking about how to problem solve by drawing on new learning from all curricular areas

Schools of social work operationalize the learning agenda differently. The school will provide you with a template. Use that template with fidelity, as the college whose student you are educating develops the learning agenda in relation to its unique social work curriculum. This allows for integration of student learning in the field with the social work curriculum, evaluation of the student's progress over time, and evaluation and accountability of the social work academic program as a whole. Different schools will have different learning agendas. Be flexible as you adapt to each college's determination of what works best for its program.

PURPOSE AND DEVELOPMENT OF THE LEARNING AGENDA

A learning agenda's main purpose is to provide a framework for student identification of needed learning, and for the evaluation of the demonstrable competencies and behaviors shown by the student at the field site. It provides clarity in roles among the student, the field instructor, and the field liaison from the college. The learning agenda is dynamic and will change as the student and agency context change. Although learning is the main thrust, other purposes of the learning agenda are explored in this section.

Universality of Social Work Education

Throughout the United States, accredited schools of social work utilize the competencies developed by the CSWE (2015). See Exhibit 4.1 for all nine competencies. These competencies create the universal framework for social work education. They provide assurance of linkages across programs and speak to the values of the profession. Most colleges and universities use these competencies as the basis for developing learning agendas in their field education programs. You will become very familiar with the competencies after instructing several social work field students. The breadth of the competencies allows for the specification of learning at each agency. Therefore, although the overarching learning is the same, the expression and demonstration of the competencies on the learning agenda are unique to the student, the agency, and the community in which you work. Consider this a strong platform for you to leap from as you help your students nuance the personal learning they plan to accomplish.

Integration of Classroom Learning and Field Experience

The learning agenda is a bridge between the classroom learning experience and the field experience (Royse, Dhopper, & Rompf, 2012). This bridge is most strongly built when there are clear opportunities for integration of classroom learning components and experiences within

EXHIBIT 4.1
Council on Social Work Education 2015 Social Work Competencies

1. *Demonstrate ethical and professional behavior*
2. *Engage diversity and difference in practice*
3. *Advance human rights and social, economic, and environmental justice*
4. *Engage in practice-informed research and research-informed practice*
5. *Engage in policy practice*
6. *Engage with individuals, families, groups, organizations, and communities*
7. *Assess individuals, families, groups, organizations, and communities*
8. *Intervene with individuals, families, groups, organizations, and communities*
9. *Evaluate practice with individuals, families, groups, organizations, and communities*

Source: Council on Social Work Education (2015, pp. 7–9).

the agency. Ask students questions that help them build that bridge for their own learning. The development of the practice behaviors requires the student to analyze relationships among courses, fieldwork, and the CSWE competencies. Invite students to bring their course syllabi. Ask students to identify major assignments. What are the connections the students can see? What can you, as field instructor, add? Be willing to include some course assignments on the field agenda, explicating the connections between field and classroom learning. What readings have they had that explore the expression of these competencies? How do they inform the work at the field site? What course assignments build on the field experiences? At every opportunity, integrate the classroom learning and the field learning as you develop the competencies. Exhibit 4.2 provides selected examples from a dozen actual student learning agendas from an undergraduate bachelor's degree in social work (BSW) program. As exemplars, they offer ideas for undergraduate and generalist activities that are measurable and aim for holistic learning in the field.

EXHIBIT 4.2
Exemplars of Competencies, Practice Behaviors, and Fieldwork Tasks

COMPETENCY	PRACTICE BEHAVIOR	FIELD TASKS
1. Demonstrate ethical and professional behavior	Use reflection and self-regulation to manage personal values and maintain professionalism in practice situations	Seek awareness of others' values, the agency's values, social work values, and my own. Self-reflect on these different values through field logs; reflect within field seminar; process and reflect on these within supervision
2. Engage diversity and difference in practice	Present themselves as learners and engage clients and constituencies as experts of their own experiences	Use the strengths to embrace difference and promote positivity to inform my practice. Use the experiences and knowledge that the clients have to further my understanding of domestic violence in families

(continued)

43

EXHIBIT 4.2
Exemplars of Competencies, Practice Behaviors,
and Fieldwork Tasks (*continued*)

COMPETENCY	PRACTICE BEHAVIOR	FIELD TASKS
3. Advance human rights and social, economic, and environmental justice	Engage in practices that advance social, economic, or environmental justice	Attend Social Work Day at the Capitol and write a letter to the editor on a chosen social justice issue
4. Engage in practice-informed research and research-informed practice	Use practice experience to inform scientific inquiry and research	Incorporate field instructor's perspective with clients and health literacy language to inform research paper for the health literacy project
5. Engage in policy practice	Identify social policy at the local, state, and federal levels that affects well-being, service delivery, and access to social services	Discuss relevant policies with colleagues that will impact our clients; discuss how we can take action and/or collaborate with outside agencies that are taking action toward policy support and reform. Attend housing/homelessness trainings and consortium meetings
6. Engage with individuals, families, groups, organizations, and communities	Continuously discover, appraise, and attend to changing locales, populations, scientific and technical developments, and emerging societal trends to provide relevant services	Attend student assistance team meetings to collaborate with other school social workers and other staff within the school environment. Observe and focus on engaging all members of the student assistance teams
7. Assess individuals, families, groups, organizations, and communities	Collect and organize data, and apply critical thinking to interpret information from clients and constituencies	Prior to interacting with individuals or groups, mentally prepare for the upcoming interaction. Discuss which skills and assessment tools to use with field instructor in advance

(*continued*)

EXHIBIT 4.2
Exemplars of Competencies, Practice Behaviors,
and Fieldwork Tasks (*continued*)

COMPETENCY	PRACTICE BEHAVIOR	FIELD TASKS
8. Intervene with individuals, families, groups, organizations, and communities	Critically choose and implement interventions to achieve practice goals and enhance capacities of clients and constituencies	Discuss possible interventions with clients and other colleagues and supervisor to identify the most appropriate intervention
9. Evaluate practice with individuals, families, groups, organizations, and communities	Critically analyze, monitor, and evaluate intervention and program processes and outcomes	Using assessment tools and results, identify areas where needs are unmet. Work with field instructor to make changes in accordance with agency mission and goals

Development of the Student Practitioner Over Time

Well-written learning agendas include developmental elements for the student. The learning agenda is a tool to identify what learning experiences the agency has to offer and what skills and abilities the student brings. Allow the student to develop the agenda, as the development is a pedagogical technique that allows students to begin to think and express themselves like a social worker (Boitel & Fromm, 2014). Remind students that the development process should be challenging, as it is representative of the growth they can expect over the course of their field experience. Guide them as they develop the agenda, but ensure that the responsibility of the development is in their hands. This responsibility and level of participation is congruent with our understanding of encouraging professional development (Fox & Zischka,1989). The student's learning agenda, along with the field instructor's close attention, is the driving force for this development. To help maximize this developmental process, use the six key questions presented in Exhibit 4.3 as you guide the student in developing a personalized learning agenda. If you can answer yes to each of the questions in Exhibit 4.3, you have a well-written practice behavior that will guide the student's field learning, enhance the client experience, and provide a useful service to the organization.

Moreover, the field site is meant to develop in the student areas in which further growth is possible. The creation of the learning agenda should keep an eye toward the future and include areas to be developed within the student. Learning agendas should include the opportunity to evaluate students over time, formatively, as it is one of the most valuable learning strategies (Hunter et al., 2015). This formative opportunity, often at midterm, guides students in developing and refining their practice skills, and prepares them for the final and summative evaluation at the end of the semester. This is essential because students must pass field placement to continue to the next educational level and graduate from the social work program.

Discrete and Holistic Learning

Balancing the tension between discrete and holistic learning should be your overarching goal and a challenge you intentionally embrace.

EXHIBIT 4.3
Six Key Questions for Learning Agenda Development

	YES	NO
1. Is the activity/behavior specific and measurable?		
2. Is the agency able to provide the necessary context to practice the learning behavior?		
3. Does it fit with the student's practice scope and skill level?		
4. Will the student learn a behavior connected to a practice competency?		
5. Can you identify a connection to the social work educational curriculum?		
6. Can the student practice the behavior multiple times, developing independence with each succession?		

Discrete learning consists of the specific skills or tasks that students complete as they fulfill the measurable components of the learning agenda (Exhibit 4.4). *Holistic learning* involves connections to the organization, the community, and the theories of social work practice that are necessary to become a skilled professional. Helping students make these connections is the crux of exemplary field experiences. To really improve field learning, we must maintain the holistic approach, and not be directed by a "fractured" approach to learning (Wayne, Bogo, & Raskin, 2006). The challenge is writing the tasks and behaviors that make these connections clear. This is the challenge of complex writing and thinking, and your goal as a field instructor is to help the student embrace this challenge and complexity.

USING THE LEARNING AGENDA DURING FIELD SUPERVISION

In all field placements, colleges and universities aim to have social workers serving as the field instructors for student learning. The CSWE requires field instructors who have degrees from accredited social work programs for at least part of field instruction and supervision because of the unique perspective and educational model of social work education. Social work's focus on integrating the classroom with the real world is a strength of social work education and the heart of social work pedagogy.

EXHIBIT 4.4
Discrete and Holistic Learning

Discrete learning: *completing forms and documentation, participating in agency activities, meeting with clients, attending meetings, etc.*

Holistic learning: *agency dynamics, culture and difference, community context, privilege and oppression, models of practice, theories of human behavior and social environments, etc.*

Integration: *flexibility, skills that can be adapted to different communities and agencies, integration of micro and macro, integration of the theoretical and the applied, complexity of thinking, individual and social change*

Regular Use of the Learning Agenda in Supervision

Nearly all schools ask their field instructors to meet weekly with students. This allows time for intentional listening by the field instructor and opportunity for integrating learning for students. Individual time is crucial for the opportunity to ask questions in an environment of learning rather than evaluation. Field instructors should require their students to attend field instruction time with an agenda of items important for them to discuss. Seeking appropriate consultation is a professional competency, and reflects the lifelong learning required in social work.

As part of this preparation, students should review the learning agenda weekly and make connections from their course curriculum to their field education experience. Ask students to describe their experiences in learning competencies, especially if you were not there to witness their work. As you continue to work together, keep returning to the learning agenda, and identify where the student has gone deeper with greater independence. Hunter et al. (2015) suggest that field instructors give specific and focused feedback, closely related to the practice behaviors, and link theory and the behaviors as much as possible. When the time comes to evaluate the student, you will be prepared to provide a quantitative and qualitative interpretation of the quality of the social work students have performed. Using the learning agenda to guide field supervision can help students ensure that they are fulfilling required practice behaviors and help you, the field instructor, to assess students' development over time.

Case Example: Using the Learning Agenda in Field Supervision: Josef is an undergraduate student in social work and is beginning his first field placement. He has some anxiety about his new field site, a shelter program for homeless youth. He wants to do well at the field site, but is new to a professional work culture. He has had part-time jobs in summer camps as a youth counselor, and volunteered with a Boys and Girls Club for one of his sophomore-year service learning projects. Josef is not sure if these experiences have prepared him for his fieldwork. Josef has three social work courses in the fall semester and is a committed student.

Tyrone has offered to be Josef's field instructor at the shelter. Tyrone is a supervisor of the youth staff, and received his BSW before competencies were ever in place. Nonetheless, Tyrone has good supervision skills he has honed over several years while working in the shelter and at a different residential setting in his previous job. Although competencies and learning agendas are new to him, he appreciates the important bridging of learning between the classroom and the field experience.

In their first visit, Tyrone gets to know Josef better. He asks questions to elicit responses that highlight the strengths Josef already brings to the field placement and begins to connect the learning at the shelter to learning experiences from Josef's previous volunteer work and summer jobs. They lay out an agenda for their second meeting. Josef is asked to bring his syllabi to their next supervision meeting and have highlighted potential connections between course assignments and field experiences.

At this second meeting, Josef begins to describe the ways in which his classroom learning will influence his field experience. Tyrone provides context and nudging for further exploration when needed. They review the learning agenda provided by Josef's college. They begin to draft learning experiences between the courses and the agency, and connect them to competencies and practice behaviors. Although this isn't completed in an orderly fashion, they know this is okay. The holistic components of learning are best expressed if they allow room for conversation that flows between and among core practice skills and theories taught in class, such as person-in-environment practice, the developmental framework, the strengths perspective, and theories on cognition.

It takes several meetings for Josef and Tyrone to have a final version of the learning agenda complete. This allows Josef about a month of learning more about the agency and the kind of fieldwork he will be completing. The connections and descriptions of the practice behaviors have become richer and fuller in this time. The field faculty liaison from the college has also given feedback, and Josef and Tyrone are now completing the learning agenda.

Learning Agendas and Evaluation

The format of evaluation embedded in the learning agendas will vary. Each school works to develop a tool meaningful to the context of its education, and broad enough to be useful to the variety of agency partners each school collaborates with. Developing a learning agenda is a challenging task, especially when student evaluation is an inherent aspect. Learning agendas serve the function of informing the progress of learning and influence the final grade for the semester. Individual colleges and universities will structure the impact of field learning on the grade received for the course. At a minimum, field instructors determine the ability to assign a passing grade (or not) for the credits connected to the field experience.

It is important to note that, like all programs, the social work educational program in which you are partnering is also evaluating the quality of the education it provides. Field education is one component of social work education that needs to be monitored and evaluated, and a common and accessible measurement tool is the learning agenda. The learning agenda of each student can be used in two distinct ways, and there also may be others. First, schools of social work use the data from learning agendas to identify students' learning of the social work competencies. Because learning agendas are often developed in response to the competencies, they are a useful tool to measure students' applied progress in this area. These data are reported in aggregate, at each level of education, creating an overall picture of how the social work program is fulfilling its educational mandate year to year. Second, schools of social work sometimes use the learning agendas to demonstrate how students combine the field experience with classroom learning. Each learning agenda completed by a student and his or her field instructor gives examples of the real-life classroom provided by the field education program. Your work is a model for the college, as it expresses the quality of the learning experience to outside stakeholders. The most obvious stakeholder is the social work accrediting body, the CSWE. Exemplars from student learning agendas can be captured and included in reaccreditation reports. Other likely audiences also include administration within the college, as well as foundations or other funding bodies for grants and program development. Identifying ways in which social work students' work with aging adults, in health care, or in community organizing may be useful data in explicating the learning and evaluation outcomes of your program, and may open opportunities for funding and specialized programming. Ask the academic institution you work with how it might use the data from student learning agendas. The content of that answer may inform you in the creation of the learning agenda you develop with each of your students.

CONCLUSION

In some ways, the field instructor is the professor of the field classroom, and the learning agenda is the syllabus. Field instructors are experts of the knowledge base, passing on the legacy of our work to the next generation. It is an area of teaching that should not be considered lightly. And although the focus has shifted to outcomes and competencies, Tapp (2011) wisely reminds us that the process of planning, monitoring, and reviewing the learning plan is as important as the final outcomes. Field instructors are empowered by the college or university to teach in the context of the real world, and stand shoulder to shoulder with social work professors. Side by side, we pass our knowledge to the next generation of social workers, and provide for them a space to consider new developments, deepen inquiries, and take our work even further as they move on to fulfill our roles.

REFERENCES

Boitel, C. R., & Fromm, L. R. (2014). Defining signature pedagogy in social work education: Learning theory and the learning contract. *Journal of Social Work Education, 50,* 608–622.

Council on Social Work Education. (2015). *Educational policy and accreditation standards for baccalaureate and master's social work programs.* Alexandria, VA: Author.

Fortune, A. E., McCarthy, M., & Abramson, J. S. (2001, Winter). Student learning processes in field education: Relationship of learning activities to quality of field instruction, satisfaction, and performance among MSW students. *Journal of Social Work Education, 37*(1), 111–124.

Fox, R., & Zischka, P. C. (1989). The field instruction contract: A paradigm for effective learning. *Journal of Teaching in Social Work, 3*(1), 103–116.

Hunter, C. A., Moen, J. K., & Raskin, M. S. (2015). *Social work field directors.* Chicago, IL: Lyceum.

Royse, D., Dhopper, S. S., & Rompf, E. L. (2012). *Field instruction: A guide for social work students* (Updated ed.). Boston, MA: Pearson Education.

Tapp, K. (2011). A competency-based contract and student assessment for implementing US Council on Social Work Education (CSWE) 2008 competencies in field education. *Journal of Practice Teaching and Learning, 10*(3), 17–36.

Wayne, J., Bogo, M., & Raskin, M. (2006). The need for radical change in field education. *Journal of Social Work Education, 42*(1), 161–169.

FIVE

Teaching Policy in Field Education

Melissa A. Hensley

Competency in social welfare policy analysis and competency in social work advocacy skills tend to be two areas where social work students, especially those wishing to pursue a clinical career, feel uncomfortable. The direct practice skills of empathic communication and collaborative problem solving come much more naturally to many beginning practitioners than writing a policy brief or speaking before a legislative committee.

Furthermore, many field instructors in direct practice settings use macro skills such as policy practice less often than more micro skills; they themselves may feel some discomfort when it comes to teaching practicum students about social welfare policy (Pritzker & Lane, 2014). If a social worker's employment setting does not emphasize knowledge of policy or involvement in advocacy, the practitioner can get "rusty" in the practice of policy advocacy and other macro skills.

It is important for all U.S. social work students to have an understanding of the basics of the American social welfare system, as well as specialized knowledge in their own area of practice. This specialized knowledge could include information about social welfare systems and policies in other countries as well. Even clinicians whose day-to-day work is focused on providing psychotherapy still need to understand how their services have been developed and maintained—and how they are paid for. Field instructors, even those whose job requirements almost exclusively involve direct practice, still need to be able to provide knowledge regarding social policy to their practicum students.

Adequate knowledge of policy in the social work context involves more than reading about a policy or program in a book or on a website. Policy practice is a social work practice method, and successful acquisition of competence in policy practice involves a variety of skills and activities, not only in the classroom setting but in the social work practicum.

BACKGROUND

There have been a few publications in the social work professional literature in recent years that have discussed the development of macro competencies in the context of field education. Regehr, Bogo, Donovan, Anstice, and Lim (2012) provide a useful framework for assessment of competencies relevant to macro practice. They discuss the importance of acquiring "meta" competencies and "procedural" competencies to enhance macro practice (Regehr et al., 2012, p. 307). Meta competencies include personal characteristics and interaction style, whereas procedural competencies involve discrete practice skills and methods. Regehr et al. (2012) used these competencies to develop a tool for assessing macro-practice abilities. The assessment tool includes competencies with direct relevance to policy-practice skills.

Pritzker and Lane (2014) conducted a survey of bachelor's degree in social work (BSW) and master's degree in social work (MSW) field instructors in the United States, and they identified barriers and facilitators that impact teaching of policy and political social work skills in the field setting. Two notable barriers involved the fact that many field

instructors considered policy-practice skills less important than clinical skills, as well as the self-perception of some field instructors that
their own skills in policy practice/political social work were not strong
enough for them to effectively teach students (Pritzker & Lane, 2014).
Pritzker and Lane also identified ways to enhance teaching in this area,
though. Social work schools and programs might consider offering
continuing education opportunities on this topic to field instructors.
In addition, field instructors can creatively use community resources
and collaborate with social work program faculty to integrate policy-
practice methods into practicum experiences (Pritzker & Lane, 2014).

In her text *Social Work Skills: A Practice Handbook*, Trevithick (2005)
discusses the importance of negotiation, mediation, and advocacy
skills for generalist social workers. In particular, Trevithick (2005)
emphasizes the importance of educating and encouraging clients to
engage in self-advocacy regarding organizational concerns as well as
relevant public policy. Policy-advocacy skills are important for social
workers in all settings, and teaching of advocacy skills (including advocacy on behalf of clients as well as empowering clients to be advocates) can happen in many diverse social work practice contexts.

THE COMPLEMENTARY NATURE OF "MICRO" AND "MACRO" SKILLS

One helpful way to promote understanding of policy practice and
other macro skills is to point out the connections between competencies
needed for direct practice and those utilized in community or policy
practice (Ruffolo, Perron, & Voshel, 2016). Both fields of practice require
the "ability to integrate and apply social work knowledge, values, and
skills to practice situations" (Council on Social Work Education [CSWE],
2015, p. 6). Engagement with communities or organizations is most effective when practitioners demonstrate good listening skills and communicate empathy with the people they are serving (Regehr et al., 2012).

Assessment takes place at both micro and macro levels of practice.
Although different kinds of information may be collected, practitioners

at both levels should work to develop a trusting relationship with the people they are interviewing, and the process of developing a written assessment—whether of a neighborhood or an individual—requires critical thinking skills as well as attunement to the expectations and desires of the identified client. Whereas collection of assessment data for an individual might involve a one-on-one interview and review of previous service records, the assessment of a community or neighborhood may involve obtaining public data about the community as well as multiple interviews with influential stakeholders. Although the process is somewhat different, the capacity to think critically about data and to encourage trusting connections with interviewees are essential for both levels of practice (Rowan, Mathis, Ellers, & Thompson, 2013).

Intervention methods will be different depending on the size of the individual or system one seeks to impact. Choosing and implementing an intervention method, in both micro and macro practice, requires knowledge of effective practice approaches and strong decision-making skills. Intervening effectively at any level of practice depends on the practitioner's ability to partner with the client or system to make substantial changes (Trevithick, 2005). In policy practice, this could involve issuing a report analyzing existing problems in a particular program or policy, writing letters to lawmakers, or organizing community members to lobby their legislators for change. In macro practice, little data exist regarding an "evidence base" for community-level interventions (Berger, 2013, p. 127), but hopefully students and supervisors can make decisions about appropriate interventions based on practice wisdom and past experience.

Likewise, evaluation at any level of practice involves the collection of data regarding the progress or the outcomes of the people or systems we are serving, and interpreting that data to understand whether our efforts were successful or satisfactory to those we serve. In the direct-practice context, this is likely to involve aspects of single-case-design research and evaluation, as well as seeking first-person feedback from people being served. With the use of empirical research techniques as well as program evaluation, data can be amassed as an evidence base in support of particular practice (Berger, 2013). In policy practice, when evaluating the effectiveness of organizational or governmental policies, social workers are more likely to consider data in the aggregate, from agency or public records. The policy-practice efforts of social workers can be evaluated by comparing advocacy goals to achieved outcomes (Pritzker & Lane, 2014). Nonetheless, the capacity to evaluate the progress of a client or the utility of a program is essential for direct practitioners as well as those working at a macro level.

When students comprehend the similarities of the skill sets that are used in different levels of practice, it often helps them to feel more comfortable as they learn policy practice.

HOW CAN FIELD INSTRUCTORS MORE EFFECTIVELY TEACH POLICY PRACTICE TO THEIR STUDENTS?

In order to effectively teach policy practice, we do need to be aware of the policies and programs that affect the work that we do. Although clinicians may not have social policy at the forefront of their consciousness in their work, chances are that the people they serve are affected by social welfare, health care, or other policies every day. When working with a student to formulate tasks and learning activities related to policy practice, it can be good to refresh our own minds regarding policies that impact clients' lives.

First, outline for yourself a short list of two to five of the major federal or state social policies that have an impact on the work that you do. For school social workers, this might include the Individuals with Disabilities Education Act or the No Child Left Behind Act. For social workers in the field of housing and homeless services, the McKinney–Vento Act may provide a place to start. For social workers in health care, the Patient Protection and Affordable Care Act has likely played a key role in service delivery.

It can also be helpful for your preparation as well as your student's learning to consider how institutional or organizational policies affect the delivery of services and the role of social work. This may be especially true in host settings, where social work services may be strictly defined. Helping students to acquire knowledge of the impact of agency-level policies will enhance their understanding of their identity as professional social workers. Agency-level policy may affect aspects of practice in diverse ways—from policies around nondiscrimination to guidelines on documentation and billing.

The field of social work has been impacted by many Supreme Court decisions, and it is helpful for students to be aware of the role of the judicial system in shaping policies and service delivery. Decisions related to reproductive rights, civil rights, and marriage equality can impact the day-to-day work of clinical as well as macro social workers.

Identifying funding sources—whether federal, state, local, or nongovernmental—is also important. Many clinical social workers may not consider the daily connections of their work to public policy, but it is likely that many of their clients are using some sort of third-party reimbursement to pay for the services they are using. This reimbursement may have been provided by a government funding source, but even if it is a private insurance plan, it is closely regulated by several levels of government. Discussing funding sources with practicum students can be helpful as well, so that students understand how services are paid for, as well as the implications of public funding cuts or cutbacks in private insurers' benefit plans.

Second, you can locate information on social welfare policies (or you can have the practicum student look up relevant information as well). As you identify reliable sources of information on policy topics, keep track of the websites of these organizations so that you can provide this direction to students (Pritzker & Lane, 2014). In particular, being aware of advocacy organizations working in your area can be helpful to you and your students. Most states have a variety of state-level advocacy organizations that issue regular "action alerts" and provide up-to-date information on changes in legislation and regulations related to a variety of issues social workers confront in their practice. For social work students, the web page for the state chapter of the National Association of Social Workers (NASW) is a good source of relevant policy information (Simonson Clark, personal communication, May 4, 2015). Child advocacy organizations, mental health advocacy groups, and housing/homelessness groups are important resources as well.

Third, work with students to help them identify the local, state, and federal policymakers who represent them. Many states have websites where individuals can enter their address and/or a zip code to obtain information about their representatives (for example, "Who Represents Me" in Minnesota: www.gis.leg.mn/OpenLayers/districts; Simonson Clark, personal communication, May 4, 2015). When students have information on their legislators, they can more easily send letters or e-mails to those representatives. In addition, obtaining information about the committees on which their legislators serve can help students to be strategic about the correspondence they send to lawmakers. This is valuable information even for students who intend to go into clinical practice, as many state- and federal-level policies, in particular, affect the way that health care and mental health services are regulated and paid for.

Fourth, work with students to develop relevant tasks and activities that will integrate the direct-practice work they are doing with effective advocacy on issues of concern to agency clients. These can include the following:

Tasks and Activities for Practice Behaviors Associated With Policy Practice

- Attend a "Day on the Hill" event for a particular social cause.
- Attend an information session sponsored by an advocacy organization.
- Facilitate a training session on advocacy for agency clients.
- Prepare fact sheets that can be used in training other social workers and students.
- Interview agency administrators to learn their perspectives on the impact of various social policies.

▨ Write a letter to the editor of a local newspaper on a social issue that affects clients at your agency.

▨ Write letters to state or federal legislators on relevant policy topics.

These kinds of tasks and activities can fulfill the requirements for CSWE Competency 5: "Engage in Policy Practice" (CSWE, 2015, p. 8)

> **Case Example:** Maddie, a senior in the BSW program at her university, was required to write a letter to the editor of the local newspaper as a course requirement for her Field Education Seminar class. Maddie had excellent direct-practice skills and greatly enjoyed her practicum with the local Sexual Assault Response Team. However, she was hesitant about writing to the paper; she did not think that the newspaper would take the opinion of a college senior seriously. Maddie discussed her concerns with her field instructor, who encouraged her to proceed with the assignment. Maddie wrote a letter to the paper highlighting the lack of services for survivors of sexual trauma in her community. Maddie's field instructor assisted Maddie in locating relevant data about rates of sexual victimization and the limited funding for services to survivors. To Maddie's surprise, the letter was published. Maddie was encouraged that others in her community cared about issues related to sexual violence and went on to contact her county commissioner as well.

DISCUSSING POLICY PRACTICE IN SUPERVISION

Field instructors should set aside time during supervision sessions to discuss what students are learning—both the content of policies themselves as well as skills associated with policy practice (Pritzker & Lane, 2014). A major integrative task of the student in social work practicum is to gain the ability to understand the impact of social welfare policy on clients and client systems, and the practicum supervision session is one setting in which students can discuss the application of their classroom learning in social policy to the work they are doing in the field.

One way to facilitate learning of policy practice is to have practicum students develop a "policy eco-map" for one of the clients they have been working with. The policy eco-map is similar to a traditional eco-map, but instead of outlining all of the environmental issues affecting a particular client or client family, the policy eco-map outlines all of the public policies that are affecting the client or client family. It can be quite revealing for students to name all of the significant policies. In many cases, clients are affected far more broadly by public policy than students truly understand at first.

CONCLUSION

Teaching social work practice skills related to public policy is an important aspect of field education. Although not all students may be interested in pursuing a career in policy advocacy, it is still important for all social work students to have a basic understanding of social welfare systems as well as knowledge of particular policies that may impact their clients directly. Field instructors can encourage students' learning in this area by discussing policies and programs in supervision. Sharing knowledge of relevant advocacy organizations and government departments can also benefit students' acquisition of policy-practice skills. Field instructors can also help students to develop and carry out tasks that will use their generalist skills to promote fair and just social policies.

REFERENCES

Berger, R. (2013). Incorporating EBP in field education: Where we stand and what we need. *Journal of Evidence-Based Social Work, 10*(2), 127–135.

Council on Social Work Education. (2015). *Educational policy and accreditation standards for baccalaureate and master's social work programs.* Alexandria, VA: Author.

Pritzker, S., & Lane, S. R. (2014). Field note—integrating policy and political content in BSW and MSW field placements. *Journal of Social Work Education, 50*(4), 730–739.

Regehr, C., Bogo, M., Donovan, K., Anstice, S., & Lim, A. (2012, Spring/Summer). Identifying student competencies in macro practice: Articulating the practice wisdom of field instructors. *Journal of Social Work Education, 49*(2), 307–319.

Rowan, N., Mathis, L., Ellers, F., & Thompson, J. (2013). Creating learning opportunities for the enhancement of critical thinking skills in BSW education. *The Journal of Baccalaureate Social Work, 18,* 123–140.

Ruffolo, M. C., Perron, B. E., & Voshel, E. H. (2016). *Direct social work practice: Theories and skills for becoming an evidence-based practitioner.* Los Angeles, CA: Sage.

Trevithick, P. (2005). *Social work skills: A practice handbook* (2nd ed.). New York, NY: Open University Press.

SIX

Integrating Theory and Practice Methods in Field Education

Laura A. Boisen and Bibiana Koh

Nearly all social work professionals remember their field instructors. Etched in their minds are the agency-based social workers who volunteered their time to mentor them and to foster their early professional growth. Even decades later, social workers can be asked about their field placement sites and their field instructors, and rich narratives will emerge. Whether their experiences were positive, negative, or mixed, it is the environment that offers the best evidence about whether one has chosen the right profession. Thus, field instructors clearly play a critical role in social work education.

The Council on Social Work Education (CSWE) has long recognized the contribution of field instructors and the essential nature of the field practicum. Consequently, field has been designated as the signature pedagogy in social work education. In assigning this designation, Pierce (2008) asserted its importance in not only socializing aspiring social workers, but also by delineating the duty of field instructors to "connect the theoretical and conceptual contribution of the classroom with the practice world of the practice setting" (p. 2).

Thus, field instructors have explicitly been given the responsibility to teach students how to bridge theories and practice. Yet this task can be daunting to some. Even the most competent practitioner can be flummoxed by how to effectively weave together the classroom content and the daily demands of professional practice in a practical and theoretical sense. To complicate matters, some field instructors may fail to see the importance of conceptualizing case information (Homonoff, 2008).

This chapter is for those field instructors who would like to broaden their repertoire of tools for helping students become more adept at integrating theory, models, and skills in a coherent manner. First, we will briefly review the literature, then identify barriers, and, finally, make recommendations about strategies for theory and practice integration.

LITERATURE REVIEW

Many academics involved in field education have described the integration of theory and practice as pivotal to the continuation of the profession (Bogo & Vayda, 1998; Mary & Herse, 1992; Munson, 1987; Risler, 1999). But for all its importance, social workers who are highly skilled in their interactions with clients can be ill-equipped to assist social work interns to identify and conceptualize cases using specific theories. Indeed, some have suggested that integrating theory and practice is one of the greatest challenges for field instructors (Murdock, Ward, Ligon, & Jindani, 2006). Numerous authors have enumerated the barriers to the transfer of classroom theory to the field practicum. They include: (1) the difficult and complex process of integration (Bogo & Vayda, 1998; Risler, 1999); (2) the disconnection students feel between the classroom and the practice setting, and students' proclivity to simply imitate their field instructors in the absence of a connection (Vayda & Bogo, 1991); (3) the increasing pressures on field instructors, such as large caseloads, productivity quotas, and dwindling resources

(Bocage, Homonoff, & Riley, 1995; Donner, 1996; Raskin & Blome, 1998); (4) more constraints facing the social work field faculty that result in less time being devoted to field instruction training (Bennett & Coe, 1998; Burke, Condon, & Wickell, 1999); and (5) a concern about the number of social work agencies willing to accept students (Skolnik, Wayne, & Raskin, 1999).

Indeed, field instructors are recruited by schools of social work for a myriad of reasons, and field instructors' motivations vary widely. In recruitment, sometimes the agency is highly sought after and the field instructor's qualifications are secondary. Optimally, the field instructor is a respected professional who is passionate and has the ability to energize and inspire students. However, in this age of declining resources, schools may be searching for a placement, any placement. If the field instructor is good at integration, this ability is a plus—but the field instructor's acumen in integrating theory and practice is rarely the reason the field instructor is recruited or assigned field students.

From a field instructor's viewpoint, motivation to mentor students can stem from a number of reasons. The field instructor may want to influence future professionals or feel a sense of professional duty (Bennett & Coe, 1998). Some practitioners desire a new challenge or want to teach (Globerman & Bogo, 2003), whereas others develop a sense of professional competence from the experience (Urdang, 1999). Agencies sometimes help motivate the social work practitioner to "volunteer," as a competent student can provide additional help to the agency (Lacerte, Ray, & Irwin, 1989) in an era of declining agency resources. Then, an already-burdened field instructor may face a multitude of responsibilities with that student—for example, selecting appropriate cases, conceptualizing and structuring an appropriate supervisory format, and evaluating the student's performance (Gitterman, 1987)—without accounting for pedagogical challenges related to theory and practice integration.

Whatever the motivation and demands, social work practitioners are as responsible for theory as field faculty (Fisher & Somerton, 2000). Short, Priddy, McChesney, Murdock, and Ward (2004) asserted that field instructors are much like classroom teachers; thus, they are inherently responsible for helping students identify and strengthen the theoretical knowledge base that will guide their practice as social workers. Given this mandate, how confident are field instructors in their ability to assist a student to integrate theory and practice?

Dettlaff and Dietz (2008) found that even those field instructors strong in theory felt insecure in this area, and both new and experienced field instructors wanted training so they could more effectively help students connect theory and practice. Homonoff (2008) studied a group of social workers who were recognized nationally for their excellence in field instruction. Most in the sample, a sample that had a deep theoretical knowledge base, believed being able to conceptualize cases theoretically was paramount to effective practice. But several acknowledged the complexity and time-consuming burden of helping students integrate theory and practice (Homonoff, 2008). In fact, some of these respondents stated that they did not focus on theory, but rather focused on models of practice in their work with students.

One interesting caveat from this study (Homonoff, 2008) was the skepticism evidenced by two of the field instructor exemplars in this sample. They questioned the merits and relevance of the need to integrate theory and practice. Indeed, Forte and LaMade (2011) found that although field instructors could identify the basic and practice theories that characterized their work, they questioned their usefulness. The authors concluded that some field instructors believe that "technique can be taught independent of theory" (Forte & LaMade, 2011, p. 89). These authors suggest that although field instructors have received an explicit mandate from the CSWE and schools of social work, some field instructors may be involuntary participants in carrying out this mission of integration.

So, what do proponents of theory-driven practice say about the importance of case conceptualization based on theory? Fisher and Somerton (2000) argue that "there is no such thing as theory-less practice" (p. 388) and that the integration of "theory and practice is central to the exercise of professional judgment" (p. 388). As do many others, they see critical reflection on one's practice as the primary mechanism in developing best practice. Indeed, without theory, the assessment and treatment process becomes a rudderless vessel. How does one know which questions are relevant to ask, which hypotheses to formulate, or the most effective practice model to employ if not drawing from theory? It may be that practitioners cannot identify the theoretical orientations that they are using, but we might also conclude that it is the rare practitioner who can provide effective services to a broad array of clients over time without a sound theoretical knowledge base.

The theory–practice integration task is complicated by conflicting or unclear definitions of theory and models in the academic literature. For instance, is the strengths-based approach (Saleeby, 2012) a theory, model, or perspective? All three descriptors can be found in the social work literature. Likewise, Coady and Lehmann (2008) describe the conundrum with Carl Rogers's client-centered approach, which has been labeled as a theory, a therapy, and a model of practice.

To add clarity for students and field instructors, some programs clearly delineate definitions of the terms *theory* and *model* (Boisen & Syers, 2004). Thus *basic theory* (sometimes referred to as grand, large, or human behavior and the social environment [HBSE] theory) can be understood as an organizing set of assumptions or propositions that can help explain human behavior (Coady & Lehmann, 2008; Forte & LaMade, 2011). *Applied* or *practice theory* infers a conceptualization that can produce behavioral change, and *practice models* are a framework, set of guidelines, or steps that direct the practitioner in helping to facilitate change (Coady & Lehmann, 2008). Those who support a theory-driven practice approach suggest that clarity of thought and coherent practice approaches are born from the ability of practitioners to conceptualize client issues from theory (Coady & Lehmann, 2008; Fisher & Somerton, 2000).

STUDENT FEEDBACK RELATED TO INTEGRATION

How do students view the integration of theory and practice? The literature suggests that students have appreciated the systematic integration of theory and practice by field instructors. In one study, Choy, Leung, Tam, and Chu (1998) found that students rated field instructors highly when they provided examples of application of theory to real-life situations. Another study found that one of the most influential teaching activities with students included not only reviewing and analyzing cases, but also integrating theory and practice in this process (Knight, 2000). Additionally, students, especially concentration-year students, valued field instruction that included the conceptualization of theory and practice frameworks and activities (Bogo, 2006). In fact, learning activities that included feedback on process recordings, critiquing one's own work, and the field instructor's intentional connection of practice and theory were positively correlated to students' positive perceptions of their field placements (Bogo, 2006).

FOSTERING INTEGRATION

Given the mounting evidence suggesting that students value integration, social work educators have used multiple strategies to help students with the integration process. Some social work programs have placed the primary responsibility of the integration process within the field seminar with the hope that field instructors will reinforce the field seminar teachings. Other programs depend almost exclusively on the field instructor's ability to achieve this goal.

The literature about how to foster integration in field education has a different focus when comparing academic field faculty and agency-based field instructors. Academic field faculty literature is two-pronged: (1) based on learning theory, pedagogical models are described that delineate a framework with specific steps and (2) teaching strategies are described. The literature related to field instructors concentrates on teaching strategies almost exclusively.

Field Faculty Models and Strategies

Programs that place the onus of integration on the field seminar and academic field faculty may utilize models such as the Integration of

Theory and Practice (ITP) loop (Bogo & Vayda, 1989, 1998) and Integrated Case Analysis Model (ICAM; Boisen & Syers, 2004) to achieve this goal. Field faculty may also use various strategies (e.g., learning logs, "theory circles," process recordings, journaling, case vignettes) to promote integration.

Notably, two of the models proposed in the field, the ITP and ICAM, require students to *first* theoretically conceptualize the case before moving to a discussion of interventions. Both models position theory at the forefront in the integrative theory–practice learning process. The ITP (Bogo & Vayda, 1989, 1998), for instance, adapted Kolb's model (1984) specifically for field education. In Kolb's (1984) model, students undergo a four-stage experiential learning process whereby they (1) experience and recall a practice situation, (2) examine the situation through reflection, (3) explain the situation by linking knowledge and theory, and (4) actively apply the feedback gained in the process to select a professional response. Similarly, Bogo and Vayda's (1989, 1998) ITP loop prescribes this four-step iterative process to analyze practitioner–client transactions and interventions until the most appropriate intervention has been chosen.

Boisen and Syers (2004) developed a more linear approach, the ICAM, which encourages students to conceptualize their case situations from a theoretical perspective. Based on a case from a student's practicum, students and faculty alike pose questions with the intent to understand the etiology of the presenting problem(s). The discussion draws upon grand theory to aid in building hypotheses and explaining relevant data, before selecting a practice theory or complementary practice model and discussing practice skills. Periodically, the theoretical underpinnings of the questions themselves are identified during the integrative discussion.

The literature also suggests several other teaching strategies for the field seminar. For instance, Gelfand (1990) presents a rationale for a learning log where student and field faculty exchange ideas and feedback throughout the practicum. The field faculty intentionally infuses theoretical conceptualization in his or her questions and feedback.

Another strategy is the "theory circle," in which the class is divided into two groups: One group conceptualizes using grand theory while the other group conceptualizes using practice theory (Collingwood, Emond, & Woodward, 2008). A third strategy involves the use of process recordings and integrative journals (Lesser & Cooper, 2006). The integrative journal, which is discussed in small groups, delineates case material from the practicum, and students are expected to identify theory as it relates to the case. Finally, vignettes are used in case-based inquiry learning groups where students are asked to develop hypotheses (Cree, McCauley, & Loney, 1998). In all of these strategies, theory is at the crux of the students' learning.

Field Instructor Strategies

The literature that pertains to how field instructors assist students with the integration of theory and practice is more focused on teaching strategies than models that offer a framework to accomplish the task. These creative strategies can be used independent of any pedagogical framework.

Some of these strategies intentionally infuse theoretical conceptualizations in the initial analysis. For instance, Hawthorne (1987) advises a "practice meets theory" dialogue between the intern and field instructor whereby students use their process recordings and relate the case information to relevant theories. Lesser and Cooper (2006) propose the use of the "clinical agenda" in the clinical supervision. In this document, students pay special heed to the emerging themes in their practice and offer the opportunity for the theoretical conceptualization to be examined.

A second set of strategies guides the field instructor through a re-examination process by the student once an issue has been identified. The "critical incident" approach is one such strategy (Fisher & Somerton, 2000; Thompson, 1995; Wright, 1989). In this approach, the field instructor or student identifies a significant incident. As the student describes the events, the field instructor infuses questions about the theory base the student is applying and how the student's understanding might change if viewed through another theoretical lens. Atkins and Murphy (1993) delineated a similar six-stage procedure whereby the student: (1) becomes aware of uncomfortable feelings or thoughts; (2) describes the situation, including thoughts and feelings; (3) analyzes knowledge and feelings related to the situation; (4) considers knowledge that was incomplete and/or helps explain or solve the issue; (5) identifies learning; and (6) implements a new action.

Finally, Clapton et al. (2008) suggested a more geographically collaborative approach between field instructors and the academic field faculty. They believe that theory and practice integration could be enhanced if the academic field faculty moved their classroom work into the field setting and widened their role to guest lecturer or on-site advisor (Clapton et al., 2008).

By this time, we are hoping that we have convinced even the most skeptical field instructor of the need to help students identify and apply theory to their practicum cases. As discussed earlier, models such as the ITP (Bogo & Vayda, 1989, 1998) and ICAM (Boisen & Syers, 2004) are pedagogical tools that underscore the importance of theory in academic settings. The wisdom of the field literature suggests that multiple teaching strategies (e.g. in-person case consultation, process recordings, critical incidents, etc.) are available to field instructors. Even with these suggested strategies and learning tools, field instructors may still feel challenged by this daunting task of integrating theory and practice.

In response, we outline a total of six recommendations to help focus field instructors' efforts and/or approaches at integration. It is important to note that the first three suggestions are not context specific—any field instructor–intern dyad could implement these recommendations regardless of the practicum setting and/or resources available. The second set of recommendations may be context specific and/or resource based (e.g., funding, time, etc.). Note that these recommendations are not mutually exclusive and may be used in tandem. Case examples are provided following each recommendation.

RECOMMENDATIONS

Universally Applicable

1. Focus on one or two theories or models: The anecdotal advice of field faculty and field instructors suggests that field instructors focus on only one or two theories or models that resonate most with the field instructor and/or student. Often, these are theories or models that align with field instructors' values and/or worldviews, or perhaps are those that they felt most comfortable with during their own social work training. Knowing a field instructor's worldview and/or theoretical leanings at the outset of a placement may help inform this process. (Note: For field instructors who state their approach is atheoretical, encourage them to talk about their approach and interventions and work backward from there. Remember that we are all implicitly or explicitly working from a set of beliefs that help guide our understanding of human behavior.)

After identifying one or two theories and models at the outset, the field instructor can then focus on these one or two rather than span many different theories and models. No one is expected to be an expert in multiple theories and models. Sacrificing breadth for depth may promote student learning.

> **Elena—Field Instructor Case Example:** Elena is a field instructor with a proclivity toward a strengths-based perspective, and a collaborative approach that focuses on the present would be a natural fit with the postmodern solution-focused practice model. At the outset of each student field placement, she shares these theoretical leanings with each student she supervises. Elena also inquires about preferred theories and models with each social work student. For students who struggle with this process, Elena will help them to identify important values and worldviews; she then helps students make connections to theories and practice models.

> **Omar—Student Intern Case Example:** Omar is a foundation-year student who inherently believes that most clients' presenting problems are best explained by the past. Although he knows little about

psychodynamic theory, he will likely draw from these theories (i.e., drive theory, self psychology, object relations, ego psychology). With the help of his field faculty and field supervisor, Omar will focus his learning on psychodynamic theory.

2. Let the context help define appropriate theories and/or models of focus: Typically, particular theories or practice models are most often demanded in a particular setting/practice context. For instance, school social work settings may invite ecological systems–based work. Because of the focus on containment in school-based settings, psychodynamic approaches may be less suitable. Domestic violence shelters may call for crisis intervention practice models that are theoretically based in both ego psychology and systems theory (Coady & Lehmann, 2008). At the beginning of the practicum, field instructors, field faculty, and interns might want to discuss the theoretical orientations and practice models that have traditionally been relevant in the setting. Thus, all can be prepared to highlight these theories and models as the student's placement begins.

> **Elena—Field Instructor Case Example**: Elena is a field instructor in an outpatient community-based health center. She selected this setting because her theoretical orientation was aligned with those of some of her colleagues at her nonprofit agency. In addition to a solution-focused model, she also sometimes uses a narrative practice model. Elena typically shares her preferred theoretical framework and practice models with social work interns who interview at her agency (prior to placement); she encourages students to inquire about theoretical and models preferences at post-MSW job interviews.

> **Omar—Student Intern Case Example**: Omar has been placed in a homeless youth shelter. As a student, Omar has had to expand his knowledge of theoretical frameworks and practice models because the short-term work he does at his placement is not conducive to longer-term clinical work that may be informed by psychodynamic theories and models. Instead, Omar's supervisor encourages students to be well versed in short-term (e.g., cognitive behavioral) and crisis intervention models. Additionally, Omar's field instructor is

not very comfortable with psychodynamic theories and models, so he has encouraged Omar to keep this at the forefront of his post-MSW learning. Omar also uses his field seminar to learn from other students who draw from psychodynamic theory. For one assignment, Omar inquired about doing a case conceptualization (written assignment) with a current client using object relations and suggesting longer-term, more intensive work. His field seminar instructor was amenable to this suggestion and it has helped Omar expand his learning.

3. Identify the student intern's learning style: As a field instructor, knowing your intern's learning style may help facilitate the theory–practice integration process. Kolb's (1981, 1984) learning theory may help assist field instructors in understanding different student learning styles. For instance, "accommodators" (Raschick, Maypole, & Day, 1998) may learn best by trying different theories and models (i.e., trial by error) in their field placement. These learners may best be described within a traditional framework of "learning by doing" in social work field education (Raschick et al., 1998).

"Divergers" (Raschick et al., 1998), who are intuitive learners, may have a harder time outlining explicit links between theory and practice models in their own social work practice. Field instructors working with these learners may assist them in their conceptualization—both verbal (e.g., in clinical supervision) and written (e.g., assessments).

"Assimilators" (Raschick et al., 1998), who lean toward abstract thinking and conceptualization, may benefit most from the use of process recordings—these will allow this type of learner to ground the theory–field integrative process in practice first (something that comes less naturally), and then later connect the practice experience to the theoretical conceptualization (a more innate skill). The use of process recordings in field education also promotes self-awareness and critical reflection, both of which are important in social work education and practice (Urdang, 2010). These types of learners may also be drawn to the ICAM model in field seminar because the model starts with first conceptualizing (i.e., formulating a hypothesis based on relevant data) and then delving into what practitioners did and/or will actually do (regarding goals, interventions, evaluation, etc.).

Finally, "convergers" (Raschick et al., 1998) are strongest with respect to practical ideas/solutions and practice application. These learners may really thrive in the discussion of interventions during case presentations/conceptualizations (e.g., with the use of the ICAM model). They will also likely complement the more abstract learners (i.e., "assimilators") in a field seminar and/or agency field setting.

Another learning distinction involves identifying circular versus linear learners. The former may best respond to "theory circles" and the ITP model, whereas the latter may respond best to the ICAM.

> **Elena—Field Instructor Case Example**: As noted earlier, Elena is a field instructor in a community-based outpatient mental health setting. She tends to be practical and has a preferred "converger" learning style. She notes that this is consistent with her worldview, theoretical leaning, and preferred practice models. She frequently struggles with students who have a predilection toward abstract thinking and conceptualization. Elena has communicated with her field faculty liaison that she doesn't feel qualified to assist students in building their theoretical knowledge base.

> **Omar—Student Intern Case Example**: As discussed earlier, Omar has been placed in a homeless youth shelter. Omar's preferred learning style is as a "diverger"—he describes himself as intuitive and drawing from his "sixth sense." If Omar were working with Elena, their challenge would be to ground Omar's clinical work in a conceptual framework. Some of the context-specific suggestions that follow may help them with this challenge.

Context-Specific and/or Resource-Based Suggestions

4. Study groups: Interns may participate in study groups to help facilitate the integrative process. Anecdotally, a college-affiliated field instructor was so successful in implementing study groups, her students continuously stood out among students as capable of integrating theory and practice. Any of the field instructor strategies discussed earlier can be used in a study group format.

> **Martha—Field Instructor Case Example**: Martha is a field instructor in a partial-day treatment program for young children, ages 3 to 8 years. The program accepts multiple interns who are assigned a specific classroom of children. There are no more than five to six children in each classroom. As part of the internship, the interns are expected to meet twice a month to discuss how they understand the development of the child's identified problematic behaviors theoretically. Thus, interns identify and apply grand theories that explain the etiology of the child's difficulties and strengths, and then delineate a coherent practice theory and model that are appropriate. Martha is available for consultation if needed, but the group is led and maintained by students.

> **Carlos—Student Intern Case Example**: Carlos was seeing a 6-year-old child who had witnessed his older brother's death by handgun. The child lived in an area of the city where parents worried about their children playing outside due to periodic, random gunshots. He lived with a single parent who struggled with substance abuse issues. The child presented with episodic aggressive behavior toward other children, dysregulation, and a desire to control his peers' behaviors. During the intern meeting, Carlos identified various grand theories that he believed influenced and explained the child's behavior (e.g., ecological, attachment, neurobiology). Carlos then drew upon cognitive behavioral theory, model, and strategies to describe his therapeutic approach.

5. Integrative field seminars: Structuring field seminars using an integrative model (e.g., ITP or ICAM) helps to facilitate students' integrative process. As noted earlier, both models underscore the importance of theory. By identifying an intern's learning style (see recommendation 3, earlier in the chapter), the appropriate model and/or strategies can be applied. By offering integration in the field seminar, students can take learning back to the field site and provide inspiration and teaching to field instructors. The next recommendation encourages bidirectional learning and cross-fertilization among field faculty, field instructors, and students.

> **Field Faculty, Field Instructor, Intern Case Example**: An intern was working in-home with a 30-year-old woman who had been held against her will by a man who physically and sexually abused her for several days 5 years prior. Due to this past trauma, the client did not leave her home. The client was hesitant to engage with the intern until they started talking about their pets; each had a dog. With the field instructor's permission, the student began to bring her dog to in-home visits. The client, accompanied by the intern, became more comfortable going outside when the dogs would need to relieve themselves. Eventually, they could all walk down the street together. Progress was being made.
>
> When the case was reviewed in the field seminar, several questions emerged from the classroom peers and field seminar instructor. Were there any liability issues related to the intern's dog? Was the dog a certified therapy dog? What were the issues regarding use of self, and the boundary implications of using one's personal pet in a therapeutic environment? Were there other ethical and liability considerations? How did this dog-companion practice fit with the theoretical conceptualization and the student's choice of practice theory and model?
>
> The student had not considered some of the issues that emerged and took the feedback to her field instructor the next week. This cross-fertilization method was effective for the field instructor, the intern, and the field faculty member as they wrestled with this unconventional approach to working with the client.

6. Integrative practice workshops: Periodically offering workshops that bring field faculty and field instructors together may help to both facilitate students' learning in the field and support field instructors in the integrative process. Dettlaff and Dietz (2008) discussed the need for field instructors to be specifically trained in a number of areas, not just offered an orientation to the college or social work curriculum.

For new or inexperienced field instructors, Dettlaff and Dietz's (2008) review of the literature suggested training in such areas as steps in structuring supervision, how to integrate adult learning theories and concepts, effective instructional methods, creating an appropriate learning environment, assessing student performance, working with challenging students, and termination (Abramson & Fortune, 1990; Bogo & Vayda, 1998; Glassman, 1995; Rogers & McDonald, 1992). For more experienced field instructors, the literature recommended training centered on topics such as enhancing students' critical thinking, group work, and communication skills, as well as conflict resolution skills (Cohen & Garrett, 1995; Dettlaff & Dietz, 2008; Glassman & Kates, 1988; Power & Bogo, 2002; Rogers & McDonald, 1992).

In an effort to garner more updated training needs, Dettlaff and Dietz (2008) conducted focus groups with field instructors to identify content they deemed essential for effective field instruction. Participants identified three broad areas of importance: (1) the mission of field education, (2) knowledge of the specific field program, and (3) expectations of student learning (Dettlaff & Dietz, 2008). More specifically, field instructors recommended training content related to effective components of field instruction, possible supervision methods, maximization of teachable moments with students, and the integration of theory with practice (Dettlaff & Dietz, 2008). Of key importance to field instructors was the preference for experiential learning activities and an opportunity to share ideas with other field instructors during the training.

Integrative Field Instructor Workshop Examples: To assist field instructors in how different personality types may influence their field instruction style, their interaction with a particular field student, and their assessment of an intern, a training session might be offered whereby field instructors take a test such as the Myers–Briggs Type Inventory (Moore, Dettlaff, & Dietz, 2004). Field instructors would outline their personality tendencies and then discuss how they have related to the student interns who have had similar or different styles.

They would also reflect on how these similarities or differences have influenced their assessment of the students' strengths and challenges.

To assist field instructors in reflecting on use of self, a workshop might focus on field instructors' definitions of use of self, how it is manifested in the field placement by the field instructor and field student, the guidance given to students about use-of-self issues, and small-group discussions of field cases where use-of-self issues have created clinical, ethical, and/or boundary crossings. The host field faculty would provide a conceptualization of use of self and cases that would highlight clinical, ethical, and/or boundary issues.

SUMMARY

In this chapter, we have attempted to highlight the key role that field instructors play in facilitating the ability of students to integrate theory and practice in the field of social work. To effectively achieve this daunting task, we have delineated a number of teaching methods that can enhance the field instructor's abilities in this area. Helping students to understand the integration of theory and practice is so challenging that the combined efforts of university field faculty and field instructors are a must.

REFERENCES

Abramson, J. S., & Fortune, A. E. (1990). Improving field instruction: An evaluation of a field seminar for new field instructors. *Journal of Social Work Education, 26*(3), 273–286.

Atkins, S., & Murphy, K. (1993). Reflection: A review of the literature. *Journal of Advanced Nursing, 18*, 1188–1192.

Bennett, L., & Coe, S. (1998). Social work field instructor satisfaction with faculty field liaisons. *Journal of Social Work Education, 14*(3), 345–352.

Bocage, M., Homonoff, E., & Riley, P. (1995). Measuring the impact of the current state and national fiscal crises on human service agencies and social work training. *Social Work, 40*(5), 701–705.

Bogo, M. (2006). Field instruction in social work: A review of the research literature. *The Clinical Supervisor, 24*(1/2), 163–193.

Bogo, M., & Vayda, E. (1989). Developing a process model for field instruction. *Canadian Social Work Review, 6,* 224–232.

Bogo, M., & Vayda, E. (1998). *The practice of field instruction in social work: Theory and process* (2nd ed.). New York, NY: Columbia University Press.

Boisen, L., & Syers, M. (2004). The integrative case analysis model for linking theory and practice. *Journal of Social Work Education, 40*(2), 205–217.

Burke, S. G., Condon, S., & Wickell, B. (1999). The field liaison role in schools of social work: A break with the past. *The Clinical Supervisor, 18*(1), 203–210.

Choy, B. K., Leung, A. Y. L., Tam, T. S. K., & Chu, C. H. (1998). Roles and tasks of field instructors as perceived by Chinese social work students. *Journal of Teaching in Social Work, 16*(1/2), 115–132.

Clapton, G., Cree, V. E., Allan, M., Edwards, R., Forbes, R., Irwin, M., . . . Perry, R. (2008). Thinking "outside the box": A new approach to integration of learning for practice. *Social Work Education, 27*(3), 334–340.

Coady, N., & Lehmann, P. (Eds.). (2008). *Theoretical perspectives for direct social work practice: A generalist-eclectic approach.* New York, NY: Springer Publishing Company.

Cohen, M. B., & Garrett, K. J. (1995). Helping field instructors become more effective group work educators. *Social Work with Groups, 18*(2/3), 135–148.

Collingwood, P., Emond, R., & Woodward, R. (2008). The theory circle: A tool for learning and for practice. *Social Work Education, 27*(1), 70–83.

Cree, V., McCauley, C., & Loney, H. (1998). *Transfer of learning: A study.* Edinburgh, Scotland: Scottish Office Central Research Unit.

Dettlaff, A. J., & Dietz, T. J. (2008). Making training relevant: Identifying field instructors' perceived training needs. *The Clinical Supervisor, 23*(1), 15–32.

Donner, S. (1996). Field work crisis: Dilemmas, dangers, and opportunities. *Smith College Studies in Social Work, 66,* 317–331.

Fisher, T., & Somerton, J. (2000). Reflection on action: The process of helping social work students to develop their use of theory in practice. *Social Work, 19*(4), 387–401.

Forte, J. A., & LaMade, J. (2011). The center cannot hold: A survey of field instructors' theoretical preferences and propensities. *The Clinical Supervisor, 30*(1), 72–94.

Gelfand, B. (1990). The reflective log: An essential teaching instrument in assisting students to integrate theory with practice in a communication skills laboratory. *Canadian Social Work Review, 7*(2), 273–282.

Gitterman, A. (1987, January 12). *Field instruction in social work education: Issues, tasks and skills.* ATRAN Lecture, Wurzweiler School of Social Work, New York, NY.

Glassman, U. (1995). Special issues in the education of field instructors. In G. Rogers (Ed.), *Social work field education: Views and visions* (pp. 185–196). Dubuque, IA: Kendall Hunt.

Glassman, U., & Kates, L. (1988). Strategies for group work field instruction. *Social Work with Groups, 11*(1/2), 111–124.

Globerman, J., & Bogo, M. (2003). Changing times: Understanding social workers' motivation to be field instructors. *Social Work, 48*(1), 65–73.

Hawthorne, L. S. (1987). Teaching from recordings in field instruction. *The Clinical Supervisor, 5*(2), 7–22.

Homonoff, E. (2008). The heart of social work: Best practitioners rise to challenges in field instruction. *The Clinical Supervisor, 27*(2), 135–169.

Knight, C. (2000). Engaging the student in the field instruction relationship: BSW and MSW students' views. *Journal of Teaching in Social Work, 20*(3/4), 173–201.

Kolb, D. A. (1981). Learning styles and disciplinary differences. In A. W. Chickering & Associates (Eds.), *The modern American college* (pp. 232–255). San Francisco, CA: Jossey-Bass.

Kolb, D. A. (1984). *Experiential learning: Experience as the source of learning and development.* Englewood Cliffs, NJ: Prentice Hall.

Lacerte, J., Ray, J., & Irwin, L. (1989). Recognizing the educational contributions of field instructors. *Journal of Teaching in Social Work, 3*(2), 99–113.

Lesser, J. G., & Cooper, M. (2006). Theory and practice: An integrative model linking class and field. *Journal of Teaching in Social Work, 26*(3/4), 121–136.

Mary, N. L., & Herse, M. H. (1992). What do field seminars accomplish? Student and instructor perspectives. *Journal of Teaching in Social Work Education, 6*(2), 59–73.

Moore, L. S., Dettlaff, A. J., & Dietz, T. J. (2004). Using the Myers–Briggs Type Indicator in field education supervision. *Journal of Social Work Education, 40*(2), 337–349.

Munson, C. E. (1987). Field instruction in social work education. *Journal of Teaching in Social Work, 1*(1), 91–109.

Murdock, V., Ward, J., Ligon, J., & Jindani, S. (2006). Identifying, assessing, and enhancing field instructor competencies. *Journal of Baccalaureate Social Work, 12*(1), 165–183.

Pierce, D. (2008). *Field education in the 2008 EPAS: Implications for the field director's role.* Retrieved March 4, 2015, from http://www.cswe.org/File.aspx?id=31580

Power, R., & Bogo, M. (2002). Educating field instructors and students to deal with challenges in their teaching relationships. *The Clinical Supervisor, 21*(1), 39–57.

Raschick, M., Maypole, D. E., & Day, P. A. (1998). Improving field education through Kolb learning theory. *Journal of Social Work Education, 34*(1), 31–42.

Raskin, M. S., & Blome, W. W. (1998). The impact of managed care on field instruction. *Journal of Social Work Education, 34*(3), 365–374.

Risler, E. A. (1999). Student practice portfolios: Integrating diversity and learning in the field experience. *Arete, 23*(1), 89–96.

Rogers, G., & McDonald, L. (1992). Thinking critically: An approach to field instructor training. *Journal of Social Work Education, 28*(2), 166–177.

Saleeby, D. (2012). *The strength perspective in social work practice.* New York, NY: Pearson/Allyn & Bacon.

Short, G. F. L., Priddy, W. W., McChesney, M.-J., Murdock, V., & Ward, J. (2004). Teaching field instructors: An education module for field instructors and educators. *Professional Development: The International Journal of Continuing Social Work Education, 7*(3), 39–51.

Skolnik, L., Wayne, J., & Raskin, M. (1999). A worldwide view of field education structures and curricula. *International Social Work, 42*(7), 471–483.

Thompson, N. (1995). *Theory and practice in health and social welfare.* Buckingham, England: OUP.

Urdang, E. (1999). Becoming a field instructor: A key experience in professional development. *The Clinical Supervisor, 18*(1), 85–103.

Urdang, E. (2010). Awareness of self—A critical tool. *Social Work Education, 29*(5), 523–538.

Vayda, E., & Bogo, M. (1991). A teaching model to unite classroom and field. *Journal of Social Work Education, 27*(3), 271–278.

Wright, B. (1989, May 10). Disasters: Critical incidents. *Nursing Times, 85*(19), 34–36.

SEVEN

Supervisory Processes: Supporting Development and Positive Change for Every Student

Melissa A. Hensley

Serving as a field instructor is usually a delightful and rewarding experience. Most of our students are bright, motivated, and eager to develop into skilled professionals. However, there are times when a practicum student may be ill-suited to the internship. In some cases, there is an unsuitable "match" between the student and the activities or organizational culture of the practicum setting. In other cases, a student may not possess the necessary skills to function effectively as a social work professional (Robertson, 2013). As field instructors, we should be actively monitoring the work of our students, so that we can provide appropriate feedback and identify situations in which a student may be struggling. Field supervision is both a process and a relationship. By understanding the nature of the process and the relationship, we can contribute greatly to students' development. We can also address challenges and problems that arise in a manner that is supportive. In addition, when needed, field instructors can assist in the "gatekeeping" process and work with students to pursue career paths that may be better suited to a student's skills and interests (Robertson, 2013, p. 98).

APPROACHES TO THE SUPERVISORY RELATIONSHIP: BACKGROUND

Several frameworks have been discussed in the social work literature about the nature of the field instructor–student relationship. These include the developmental model, attachment-based approaches to supervision, and the relational approach. With all models for understanding field instruction, the importance of professional socialization is emphasized (Weiss, Gal, & Cnaan, 2008).

A developmental model of supervision can be helpful in tailoring the field instructor–student relationship to the needs and skills of the particular student. According to Everett, Miehls, DuBois, and Garran (2011), the practicum tasks and the process of supervision can be organized in a series of stages, with each stage addressing particular developmental and learning needs of the student at that time. Beginning students with little work experience may need more structure and reassurance. Advanced students can work more independently, while using supervision to discuss interventions and progress in skill development (Everett et al., 2011).

Bennett and Saks (2006) offer a conceptual framework for the field instructor–student relationship that is based on attachment theory. They emphasize that a supportive supervisory relationship is one of the main factors that facilitates learning and skill acquisition. Bennett and Saks emphasize the need for social work field instructors to provide a "secure base" and a "safe haven" for students (2006, p. 669). When the supervisory relationship is characterized by safety and mutual trust, students' capacity to process and learn from their experiences is greatly enhanced.

Recent scholarship on the topic of social work field education has emphasized the benefit of a relational approach to field instruction. Ornstein and Moses (2010) describe the relational approach as "maintain(ing) the delicate balance between a therapeutic and an educational stance in their work with students" (p. 101). When practicum students struggle with the tasks and expectations of the internship, it can be beneficial not only to consider the nature of the activities in the practicum, but also to fine-tune the nature of the supervisory relationship (Ornstein & Moses, 2010).

These frameworks for understanding the supervisory relationship are not necessarily mutually exclusive; all place a high priority on communication and mutual respect in the field instructor–student relationship. In some instances, for example, with a younger, less experienced student, a developmental approach may take priority, whereas with a student who is in the process of learning new counseling skills, a relational or attachment-based approach may seem more suitable.

HOW DO I IDENTIFY AREAS IN NEED OF IMPROVEMENT?

No practicum student is going to perform every activity perfectly the first time. Students pursue social work education because they want to learn new skills and build on their existing competencies. Field instructors should support students in learning new skills, but we should also recognize when students are struggling to learn a new skill or set of knowledge. It is important that we have a process in place for observing and evaluating students' performance, so that we can provide supportive feedback (Royse, Dhopper, & Rompf, 2012). Feedback on practice behaviors should be an integral part of supervision (Williams, 2013).

Use the learning assessment as your guide—what are the practice behaviors that the student has contracted to learn, rehearse, and utilize (Williams, 2013; also see Chapter 4 for more guidance on learning assessments)? There is no need to wait until the midterm evaluation to consult the learning assessment and measure progress. Are there behaviors that the student practices very skillfully? Are there behaviors that the student needs to develop and improve? Tracking the practice behaviors that the student outlined in his or her assessment can help you monitor the student's learning. A student may start out rehearsing a certain practice behavior and can then move into using that technique in client interactions. Some initial discomfort is to be expected when a student first learns a new skill. You will want to monitor students as they practice a skill—their level of comfort and competence should improve. If there is not improvement in a student's confidence and capabilities, this should be discussed. Although supervision should offer a "safe haven" for the student, it should also be a place where you can honestly discuss with students areas for future skill development (Bennett & Saks, 2006, p. 669).

Try to strike a balance between emphasizing strengths and pointing out areas for further growth and improvement. Honesty is the best policy. If a student is behaving in ways that are not appropriate for the practice setting, the student needs to know. It is not safe to assume that students are necessarily aware that their behavior is not suitable. If a student is struggling to learn and integrate certain practice skills, then the areas for improvement need to be pointed out clearly and directly. Using a relational approach during supervisory sessions can help the field instructor work with the student in a collaborative way (Ornstein & Moses, 2010).

Ask students for their own observations regarding their strengths and challenges. By eliciting students' own views on their progress, the field instructor can better understand students' intellectual and emotional reactions to their work in the field (Ornstein & Moses, 2010). Students may have a clear sense of what they need to improve, but are reluctant to bring up their ideas for fear that their "weaknesses" will be magnified and criticized by the field instructor. Creating a safe supervisory environment where students can honestly discuss their observations and perceptions benefits students and the field instructor (Bennett, Mohr, Brintzenhofeszoc, & Saks, 2008).

The field seminar faculty and the field education coordinator are your friends. Being upfront and transparent with college/university faculty will help because you can work together with the faculty to devise plans for student improvement (see Chapter 8). In addition, if a student is experiencing difficulties, it can be helpful to communicate with the field seminar faculty or other school representative to get a sense of whether the student is struggling only in the practicum or whether the issue is more widespread (Tully, 2015).

Working with students to improve particular skills sometimes involves closer supervision and observation of students' work. If the student can identify two or three behaviors each week to practice and reflect upon, this can help shape students' efforts to improve their performance.

Observing students as they interact with clients can be helpful in identifying strengths and challenges. If being directly observed causes anxiety for the student, then audio or video recording of student–client interactions can be helpful as well (with consent from the client, of course). New technology has made these kinds of recordings easier than ever (Danowski, 2012).

Program faculty can also work with you to help in the process of integrating classroom knowledge and theory with interventions in the practicum setting. Sometimes students may excel academically but feel quite anxious in face-to-face interactions at the practicum (Williams, 2013). It is beneficial to work together with faculty to help students translate their academic success into viable practice skills. Critical thinking and self-reflection can guide a student to better performance in the field.

COMMON "TROUBLE SPOTS"

Some areas where students may particularly struggle are the following:

- Emotional self-care
- Professionalism
- Setting appropriate professional boundaries
- Integrating classroom knowledge with fieldwork
- Professional writing skills
- Accepting constructive feedback
- Asking for help

Emotional Self-Care

Graduate school can be a very busy and stressful time. Many students have to juggle family responsibilities with paid work, classes, and practicum. This can leave students with little time for sleep and other self-care practices. Students may feel "stressed out" or overwhelmed as they try to balance their roles and tasks. Field faculty as well as field instructors and task supervisors should encourage students to try to strike a balance—to ensure that responsibilities are being met, but also to acknowledge that care for the self is essential to being able to fulfill these other roles (Danowski, 2012).

One particular area of difficulty for students is sleep deprivation. Students may try to "pull all-nighters" to complete papers for school and then report to their internship without having had adequate rest. Field instructors as well as course instructors should emphasize the danger of procrastination and encourage students to use time management skills such as "to-do" lists to help students stay on track.

> **Case Example:** Brad, a clinical social worker at a children's mental health agency, was working with Michelle, a second-year master's degree in social work (MSW) student in the clinical concentration at her university. The practicum started smoothly; Michelle had solid basic skills for direct practice with children and youth and worked well with her colleagues. However, several weeks into the practicum, Brad noticed that Michelle was "nodding off" in clinical team meetings. She also appeared increasingly disorganized and anxious. Brad was reluctant to confront Michelle because she did have such strong clinical skills, but he decided in supervision to ask Michelle if she was experiencing personal issues that were hindering her optimal performance. Michelle became tearful and mentioned that she was having difficulty establishing a balance between school, work, and her personal life. She had been frequently staying up until 1:00 or 2:00 in the morning to complete readings and papers

for school. Brad asked Michelle if she felt that creating a better balance and getting more sleep would be possible. Michelle was skeptical, but Brad arranged for Michelle to meet and talk with another agency social worker who had recently graduated from an MSW program, to discuss ways to accomplish necessary tasks while also practicing self-care. Michelle began using her smartphone to organize her tasks, appointments, and family responsibilities, and although she still struggled with fitting in all of her responsibilities, she was able to avoid all-night study and writing sessions. She was able to be more emotionally present for her clients as well as more attentive in meetings and supervision.

There may be situations in which a student is experiencing significant mental health symptoms. In this case, you want to provide supportive supervision while keeping in mind that your role with the student is not clinical. For a student struggling, for example, with depression or anxiety, you can support the student while encouraging the student to seek assistance from an on-campus counseling center or other mental health service provider. Campus counseling centers can be particularly helpful for free, short-term counseling. They also can frequently assist with referrals to other low-cost community resources. It is important to emphasize to students that when they seek mental health treatment for themselves, it is not a sign of weakness, nor does it indicate in any way that they are not suitable for a career in social work. In fact, attending to personal needs and seeking insight into one's own emotions and behaviors can be seen as a strength. Students who acquire skills in self-awareness through their own therapy process can actually use these skills to be more conscientious practitioners (Lehmann, personal communication, May 6, 2015).

In some situations, a student's emotional distress may be brought on by experiences in the practicum that trigger a strong emotional response. This is especially likely in settings where clients have experienced violence, or in settings with children or adults with severe mental health symptoms. Being able to develop coping strategies for triggering experiences is an important practice skill (Royse et al., 2012). In most cases, the development of awareness and skills related to emotional triggers is a practicum task that students refine over the course of their internship experience. As mentioned earlier, the experience of emotional triggers does not, by itself, indicate that a student should or should not pursue a social work career. However, students in all areas of social work will need to use supervision and self-reflection to understand the presence of triggers and how responsible practitioners cope with triggers in the work setting. If students are not able to deal effectively with triggers, the field instructor will want to collaborate with the student to help develop workable boundaries and management strategies. In circumstances in which students are not able to learn skills to handle triggers, you, as field instructor, along with the field education seminar faculty, may need to discuss with the student whether a different placement is needed, and, in some cases, whether social work is an appropriate career choice.

Professionalism

It is relatively rare for social work practicum students to have no paid work experience whatsoever. Even with undergraduate social work interns, students have usually had some sort of summer or after-school job, or at the very least a relevant volunteer or service learning experience. Students should be expected to understand and adhere to the basic expectations of a professional workplace.

Students should be responsible for keeping track of the number of practicum hours they have completed. At many agencies, students log this information themselves, and the agency does not involve itself in tracking hours completed. At other agencies, a time card or sign-in/sign-out system may be used. Whatever the process, students are responsible for this information.

Students should arrive to the practicum site on time, and they should notify their supervisor and/or field instructor if they are to be absent or late for any reason. If students are consistently late, this should be discussed in supervision. Students may need to allow more time for their commuting or may need to adopt better time management skills.

Students should be expected to be at their practicum site on the days and times that they have agreed to attend. If students are sick or have some sort of emergency, they need to notify the field instructor as soon as they know they will not be able to come to the practicum. Field instructors should hold students accountable for their attendance—students cannot learn practice skills if they do not show up. Persistent problems with attendance should definitely be brought up with the field seminar faculty or the college/university's field education director.

As mentioned in Chapters 2 and 3, social work practicum students should be held to the same standards as agency employees when it comes to dress, language, and interaction with clients.

When addressing issues related to professionalism at the practicum, bringing up these topics in individual supervision can often be sufficient. You can bring up areas of concern and work with the student to agree on standards for improvement. As with many challenges students encounter, concerns about professional conduct should be addressed sooner rather than later. In this way, the student can demonstrate understanding of expectations and improvement in areas where the student is struggling.

Setting Appropriate Professional Boundaries

Boundary setting is an important component of emotional self-care. In many social work settings, students may see the worst of human nature—they will encounter people who have been abused; people who suffer from severe medical illnesses, addictions, or mental illnesses; and people living in extreme poverty—just to name a few. It is human nature to be emotionally affected by these encounters, but students will benefit from learning skills that help them to acknowledge the emotional reaction and be able to let it go. Students who ruminate on clients' problems or tend to think a great deal about the practicum when they are not at the internship will be prone to higher levels of anxiety, as well as burnout (Danowski, 2012).

Many students who pursue degree programs in social work do so because at some point in their own lives they have received social services or health care services that were helpful. They are motivated to become social workers so that they can "give back" (Lehmann, personal communication, May 6, 2015). Social workers with lived experience are often excellent practitioners. There may be times, though, when social work students with lived experiences may need help in establishing a healthy practice relationship between their own experiences and their professional role (Mowbray, 1997). Many practitioners, whether or not they themselves have been social work clients, need reminders that just because an intervention worked well or makes sense for them does not mean it is a good fit for everyone. Students with lived experiences may also benefit from guidance about healthy self-disclosure (Walters, 2008).

Integrating Classroom Knowledge With Fieldwork

As discussed in Chapters 5 and 6, the capacity to integrate intellectual knowledge with practice skills is an essential social work competency (Council on Social Work Education [CSWE], 2014). Students should be able to put their knowledge of theories, methods, and social work values into a practice framework. When students are not able to discuss ways that their course content relates to the work they do in the internship, they may need some additional guidance in supervision. Students may need to engage in more structured activities to help them understand, for example, how theories of human behavior may affect the way that a particular client's challenges are dealt with in the field setting.

Professional Writing Skills

Although we would hope that students would have well-developed writing skills by the time they reach their junior year in college, or by the time they reach graduate school, unfortunately, many students in social work educational programs do not write well (Ames & Fitzgerald,

2015). Students may struggle with grammar or spelling, or they may not understand the expectations of professional writing. Even students whose basic writing skills are adequate may need some training in areas of professional writing, such as developing assessments and treatment plans or maintaining ongoing clinical documentation. Students in generalist or macro-practice settings may need additional instruction in preparing reports, policy analyses, or grant applications.

Students who lack professional writing skills can be helped in a number of ways. Students can be referred to training workshops on professional writing, or field instructors can recommend books, such as Ames and Fitzgerald's text (2015), to provide guidance to students. Some colleges and universities have writing labs, where students can go to receive proofreading help and other feedback on their writing. These labs tend to be more helpful for the development of academic writing skills rather than the professional writing tasks that students need to master in their practica. However, they can provide a starting place for students who need further writing instruction.

> **Case Example:** Martha was a clinical social worker who supervised practicum students from several different schools of social work. Martha was working with Jill, a foundation-level intern who had come to her MSW program with a bachelor's degree in psychology from a nearby college. Martha spent a great deal of time observing Jill and discussing social work tasks and roles. Although Jill had excellent communication skills in her interactions with colleagues and clients, Martha noticed that Jill's written communication skills were poor, leading to difficulties in writing client progress notes as well as assessment and treatment plan documents. Martha mentioned this concern to Jill, and Jill agreed that professional writing was a struggle for her. In conjunction with Jill's faculty field liaison/seminar instructor, Martha helped Jill to improve her writing skills. Martha and Jill included time in their supervisory meetings to go over assessments and other documents Jill had written. Jill began

consulting with the writing lab at her university and made use of a writing textbook designed for human service professionals. By the midterm evaluation, Martha was able to report to the faculty field liaison that Jill's writing had improved substantially.

Accepting Constructive Feedback

The social work practicum is intended to be a place where students can learn and practice new skills and techniques. Even if students have come into the practicum setting with a number of useful practice skills, there is still a great deal that students need to learn while they are in their field experience.

Because no student will ever practice every skill perfectly, students will need to receive feedback—both positive and negative—about their performance. Usually, the field instructor and the student will have developed an honest, trusting relationship that will encourage realistic feedback on the student's performance. However, there are times when students have difficulty receiving constructive feedback. Students may tend toward perfectionism, or they may feel so insecure in their practice skills that hearing criticism feels painful and degrading.

It is important to normalize the experience of receiving constructive—and, at times, negative—feedback. The capacity to accept and learn from criticism is a skill that social workers need not only when they are in their formal education, but also when they join the professional workforce. When a student is struggling to receive constructive feedback, you can work with the student to develop tools for coping with strong emotions or feelings of insecurity. In addition, you can assist students by reinforcing the fact that even seasoned professionals can learn and grow when they receive feedback on their performance.

Asking for Help

Students may be reluctant to ask for help when they begin their practica. They may feel intimidated by the field instructor or other agency staff and fear being reprimanded if they ask for advice or clarification.

The field instructor can be of great help to students simply by working to create an organizational culture in which it is acceptable to ask for advice or consultation when questions arise. Having this atmosphere of openness ensures that students are getting the information and training they need for professional practice (Bennett et al., 2008).

HELPING STUDENTS TO IMPROVE

Bosch, in Chapter 8 of this book, discusses at length the role of field education evaluation in helping students to improve. As a field instructor who is engaged in ongoing observation and monitoring of the practicum students' activities, you will want to provide feedback related to students' performance not only at the time of the formal midterm or final evaluation, but throughout the course of the practicum. If students are exhibiting inappropriate behaviors or are not improving in their practice skills, a mid course plan for improvement may need to be put in place. If your agency setting already has a policy and format in place for addressing performance challenges, this format can often be used with a practicum student.

Be sure to communicate with the field faculty or field education director at the student's school about such mid course performance concerns as well. Field faculty or other instructors may be able to help reinforce certain skills and knowledge in the classroom setting, which will enhance students' capacity to perform well in the practicum.

WHEN IS IT APPROPRIATE TO "FIRE" A PRACTICUM STUDENT?

Unfortunately, there are some situations in which a practicum student is unable to demonstrate improvement in performance, despite extensive support and training. If you have worked with a student to address areas of unsatisfactory performance, identifying specific behaviors in need of improvement, and the student has not improved sufficiently, then you may need to discontinue the practicum placement. This is especially true if the student is lacking in effective communication skills, is inattentive to ethical concerns such as appropriate boundary setting, or demonstrates an unsatisfactory work ethic (Robertson, 2013).

If you suspect that this may be necessary for a particular student, it is important to communicate these concerns to the student's social work program as soon as possible. Field faculty as well as field education directors will be eager to help you work with the student toward performance improvement. If a student is not improving, then letting the college/university know promptly will help the field education director as he or she considers the feasibility of the student's continuation in the program and whether to seek an alternative practicum placement for the student. It can be helpful to have an "exit interview" with a student who is leaving your agency and the student's faculty field liaison. This can help you and the student establish closure, and it can help you to communicate to the student and faculty the areas in which the student needs to improve for professional practice.

CONCLUSION

The supervisory relationship between field instructor and student is the "location" in which much of the student's learning and skill acquisition takes place. Through formal supervision sessions, as well as ongoing mentoring, observation, and feedback, students learn professional behavior, ethical standards, and relevant practice techniques. Field instructors who work with their students to develop new skills, and who provide regular, honest feedback to practicum students, play an indispensable role in students' development. Several frameworks for understanding and structuring the supervisory relationship can help field instructors adapt their supervisory style and content to the learning style of a particular student.

Even with students who are intelligent and skilled, problems can arise in the practicum. A proactive approach to students' concerns can help ensure that students receive the necessary assistance and are able to have successful experiences in the field.

ACKNOWLEDGMENT

Barbara Lehmann, PhD, LICSW, by stimulating the author's creative thinking about effective supervisory processes, had an inspiring influence on the content of this chapter.

REFERENCES

Ames, N., & Fitzgerald, K. (2015). *Writing clearly for clients and colleagues: The human service practitioner's guide*. Chicago, IL: Lyceum.

Bennett, S., Mohr, J., Brintzenhofeszoc, K., & Saks, L. V. (2008, Spring/Summer). General and supervision-specific attachment styles: Relations to student perceptions of field supervisors. *Journal of Social Work Education*, 44(2), 75–94.

Bennett, S., & Saks, L. V. (2006, Fall). A conceptual application of attachment theory and research to the social work student–field instructor supervisory relationship. *Journal of Social Work Education*, 42(3), 669–682.

Council on Social Work Education. (2014, October). *Draft 3 of the 2015 Educational Policy and Accreditation Standards*. Washington, DC: Author.

Danowski, W. A. (2012). *In the field: A guide for the social work practicum* (2nd ed.). Boston, MA: Pearson Education.

Everett, J. E., Miehls, D., DuBois, C., & Garran, A. M. (2011). The developmental model of supervision as reflected in the experiences of field supervisors and graduate students. *Journal of Teaching in Social Work*, 31(3), 250–264.

Mowbray, C. T. (1997). Benefits and issues created by consumer role innovation in psychiatric rehabilitation. In C. T. Mowbray, D. P. Moxley, C. A. Jasper, & L. L. Howell (Eds.), *Consumers as providers in psychiatric rehabilitation* (pp. 45–65). Columbia, MD: International Association of Psychosocial Rehabilitation Providers.

Ornstein, E. D., & Moses, H. (2010). Goodness of fit: A relational approach to field instruction. *Journal of Teaching in Social Work*, 30(1), 101–114.

Robertson, J. S. (2013). Addressing professional suitability in social work education: Results of a study of field education coordinators' experience. *Journal of Practice Teaching and Learning*, 11(3), 98–117.

Royse, D., Dhopper, S. S., & Rompf, E. L. (2012). *Field instruction: A guide for social work students* (Updated ed.). Boston, MA: Pearson Education.

Tully, G. (2015). The faculty field liaison: An essential role for advancing graduate and undergraduate group work education. *Social Work with Groups*, 38, 6–20.

Walters, H. B. (2008). *An introduction to use of self in field placement*. Retrieved January 26, 2015, from http://www.socialworker.com/feature-articles/field-placement/An_Introduction_to_Use_of_Self _in_Field_Placement/

Weiss, I., Gal, J., & Cnaan, R. A. (2008). Social work education as professional socialization. *Journal of Social Service Research, 31*(1), 13–31.

Williams, K. (2013). *Field placement: What students need from their field supervisors: A student's perspective.* Retrieved September 18, 2015, from http://www.socialworker.com/feature-articles/field-placement/Field_Placement%3A_What_Students_Need_From_Their_Field_Supervisors%3A_A_Student's_Perspective/

EIGHT

Field Evaluation for Professional Development

Lois Bosch

According to the Council on Social Work Education (CSWE), the field practicum is the signature pedagogy of the student's social work education. Knight (1996) suggests, "field work is the primary mechanism through which students learn to translate theoretical knowledge into practice skills" (p. 399). Considering the field practicum importance as an equal partner in learning with the academic setting, it is not surprising that considerable weight is placed on the field practicum evaluation as a part of the overall social work student portfolio. As with any academic social work course, students are evaluated on their performance in the field practicum. This chapter focuses on the use of field evaluation measures to characterize the student's readiness for social work practice.

LITERATURE REVIEW

Studies have named the merits of the fieldwork experience in social work education (Knight, 1996; Peleg-Oren, Macgowan, & Even-Zahav,

2007). Specifically, the opportunity to practice one's use of social skills and apply one's social work values in a social work context while observed by an expert is regarded as a key element of the social work learning experience. The field assessment remains a cornerstone of the social work academic program's determination of whether a student can practice social work competently. However, in conducting fieldwork assessments, challenges are acknowledged. Although the field education experience has been a prominent learning opportunity for bachelor's degree in social work (BSW) and master's degree in social work (MSW) students (Cleak, Hawkins, Laughton, & Williams, 2015), concerns emerge about the quality of the assessment experience.

One challenge to the fieldwork assessment process is the field experience itself. Field supervisors provide practice experience for students in a variety of ways that may not yield equally consistent learning opportunities across field agencies, with varying levels of expected performance and independence (Wayne, Bogo, & Raskin, 2010). This lack of uniformity may make assessment of practice preparation inconsistent and unreliable.

A second challenge to the assessment process is the multifaceted role of the fieldwork supervisor. Fieldwork supervisors act as mentors, advisors, and evaluators. Fieldwork supervisors may feel uncomfortable assessing student performance and may prefer the role of advisor and mentor to beginning social workers in their "on-the-job" experience. The role of fieldwork instructor as evaluator may promote a values conflict (Bogo, Regehr, Power, & Regehr, 2007) because the evaluation process can involve transmitting negative messages to the student and can contribute to an image of the field instructor as judging rather than guiding the student's practice performance.

A third challenge to the value of field assessment is the quality of the field assessment instrument. With the advent of the CSWE's core competencies, student behavior at the field agency is measured using competencies or discrete behavioral elements. Measuring these competencies requires that the field instructor observe clinical or social work behaviors as separate and distinct tasks or activities (Chui, 2010;

Regehr, Bogo, Regehr, & Power, 2007). However, the actual practice of social work is acknowledged to be greater than the sum of its parts. Social work practice requires the student to apply skills appropriately, in the appropriate time and place and in the appropriate way. Attending to skills, values, and knowledge as discrete elements can be seen as unduly reductionist (Chui, 2010) and overlooks the holistic, integrated nature of social work practice.

Finally, the practice of assessment can be biased or flawed (Kadushin & Harkness, as cited in Tsui, 2005). These flaws include the "halo effect" (one area of practice overshadows all other areas of performance), the "leniency effect" (the fieldwork supervisor tolerates subpar behavior, in the hopes that the student's behavior will improve), the "recency effect" (the most recent behavior adjacent to the assessment date is more heavily considered), "contrast error" (comparing one worker to another), and the "negativity effect" (it's easier to remember negative behaviors than positive behaviors) (Tsui, 2005, p. 65). All of these potential flaws can bias or unduly contaminate the assessment process, and therefore the field instructor may fail to appropriately judge the student's practice skills, knowledge, and values. In the view of these challenges, it is important that you, the field instructor, understand field learning assessment instruments, the process of assessment, and the challenges that accompany this process.

WHAT IS FIELD ASSESSMENT?

The field practicum provides students with the opportunity to apply and demonstrate the skills, knowledge, and values they have acquired in the classroom. Additionally, the field evaluation process affords students the opportunity to reflect on their practice and make adjustments as necessary. According to the National Association of Social Workers (NASW), the field evaluation includes the following: a "formal agreement between the supervisor and supervisee regarding expectations," clear goals for learning, "specific guidelines to evaluate the supervisee's performance, a time frame for goals attainment," and a discussion of possible next steps (NASW, 2013, p. 25). For the supervisee, it is considered a "valuable measurement of their achievement, which will help them to attain future professional growth" (Tsui, 2005, p. 65).

The role of the field supervisor or field instructor is complex. In addition to the role as professional mentor, the field instructor is expected to teach skills, connect theory to practice, connect research to practice, support student reflection, and balance the needs of the agency and clients with those of the student (Homonoff, 2008). The pace and expectation seem almost dizzying, and it is small wonder that being a field instructor takes a generous bite out of your work schedule. The responsibility for thoughtful evaluation adds another layer of expectation on the field agency and you, the field instructor.

The field evaluation document is an instrument that measures the student's learning over a given period of time. In those programs where the student is engaged in concurrent field placements, this is accomplished usually over the course of two semesters. In a block field placement, learning is accomplished within a more concentrated form, with a full-time assignment over the course of a few months. In either case, the fieldwork assessment takes place twice over the course of the placement, at the midterm (when the student is halfway through the internship hours), and at the end of the final term when the student has met all proposed internship tasks. Typically, the social work program designs the field evaluation form and process. The field evaluation form is fleshed out by the student and shared with the field instructor, as evaluator, for feedback and comments.

Most MSW programs incorporate the CSWE 10 core competencies to shape the field evaluation form. These competencies provide an "outcome performance approach to curriculum design" (CSWE, 2008, p. 3). The 10 core competencies span student learning over the duration of the field placement and are specifically tailored to the appropriate level of learning required, for example, BSW, MSW Foundation, and MSW Concentration. These 10 core competencies assess the students' performance in the areas of professional identity development; ethical decision making; critical thinking; engaging diversity in practice; the advancement of human and social/economic justice; development of research-informed practice and practice-informed research; the application of human behavior theories; policy practice; response to practice contexts; and the capacity for engagement, assessment, intervention, and evaluation with systems of all sizes. Each core competency is then followed by specific practice behaviors that articulate how to observe and demonstrate core competencies. The CSWE has outlined many of these practice behaviors.

Furthermore, there is a level of congruence between the student's learning contract and the field evaluation. Based on the 10 core competencies established by the CSWE, the academic program derives practice behaviors that will demonstrate and measure student learning. The student, in collaboration with the field instructor and the academic program field liaison, develops the tasks that will demonstrate the student learning. The student demonstrates each practice behavior through specific learning tasks. The student also specifies the ways that these tasks will be observed and otherwise measured—field instructor observation, documentation, discussion of activity in supervision, review of research, relevant recordings, and so on. This development of learning tasks serves as the construction of the student's learning contract and is directly measured by the fieldwork evaluation forms.

WHAT IS THE PURPOSE OF FIELD EVALUATION?

The midterm and final evaluations are incorporated into the field learning assessment and serve to inform students of how they are doing in the placement. It is the field instructor's way of communicating with students regarding where they are successful and where they need to improve. If the student has created the learning agenda or assessment, it will dovetail nicely with the assessment/evaluation protocol and create opportunities for you to review the activities the student has engaged in and how well the student has done with the activities.

As the field instructor, you are in the position to develop and monitor much of the student's capacity to interact successfully with clients. Social work is the understanding of the person in the person's environment. As such, the term *clients* includes individuals, families, groups, agencies, and communities, depending on the student's placement and learning plan.

WHAT IS THE TIMELINE?

The CSWE expects accredited programs to require students to complete at least 420 hours for the BSW student practicum, 900 hours for a Foundation MSW student practicum, and 480 hours for the Advanced Standing student practicum. As mentioned earlier, the usual time frame for a field placement depends on the program's orientation. Some programs use block practicums for their students, meaning that the student generally spends 30 to 40 hours per week in the field agency. The expectation is that students will have completed at least some of their coursework before they engage with the field experience. Other social work programs require their students to complete concurrent field practica. This means that students are taking courses side by side with their field placements. In either case, it is important that you, as the field instructor, pay attention to the following questions: When are students expected to start their placements? How many hours will they be completing each week? When is the projected completion date? These timeline expectations are important for at least two reasons: They ensure that the field instructor is aware of when the student is expected to be at the field agency, and that the field learning contract operates along an expected trajectory. Finally, the field instructor should understand the responsibilities and roles of the *faculty field liaison*, that is, the academic faculty member (from the school) who bears responsibility for administering the academic grade.

WHERE IS THE EVIDENCE?

With the use of competencies in social work education, students must discover tasks that they perform at the field agency that will demonstrate their mastery of the required skills, values, and knowledge. Those tasks serve as evidence that the student has mastered (or has not mastered) the content of the field placement. Examples of such tasks are engagement with clients, maintaining electronic records in accordance with the guidelines of the Health Insurance Portability and Accountability Act (HIPAA), and collaboration with staff and clients to create a client satisfaction survey. The evidence that shows the results of those tasks then takes a variety of forms, such as field instructor observation, process recordings of client interactions, discussion of activity in supervision session, or other relevant recordings in client files or journals. As discussed in Chapter 4, the construction of the field assessment document provides a place for listing tasks and activities that the student should complete.

WHAT COMPLICATES THE ASSESSMENT PROCESS?

So, what happens in real life? As outlined in the literature review earlier in this chapter, there are challenges to the assessment process. Bogo et al. (2007) suggest that there are four challenges in evaluating a student's field performance. The first is the correct understanding and use of the evaluation instruments. Based on your interaction with the faculty field liaison, you should understand at the beginning of the term how you are expected to report student progress. Many assessment tools are concrete and measure specific skills, behaviors, and values. For example, in assessing the student's ability to conduct ethical decision making, one suggested practice behavior is "appropriately applies strategies of ethical reasoning to address the use of technology in clinical practice and its effect on client rights" (CSWE, 2010, p. 4). This practice behavior is then measured by a specific practice task, for example, "the student will maintain electronic charts in accordance with HIPAA guidelines."

Everett, Miehls, DuBois, and Garran (2011) suggest that field instructors have different supervisory styles depending on the level of student learning (BSW, MSW Foundation, and MSW Concentration) required. Likewise, the level of evaluation is comparatively different at each level of learning. At the BSW level, most students are assumed to focus on generalist practice and be exposed to many different levels of social work practice within one placement. The BSW student would be expected to learn about how to influence the context of the individual client setting. At the MSW Foundation level, this is also the case; however, the field instructor is preparing the MSW student for the role of *independent* professional practice. Although the first half of the MSW Foundation practicum term might be spent in understanding the role of the social worker through observation and shadowing other professionals, by the second half of the Foundation placement, the student should begin the work of the professional and demonstrate the necessary skills, values, and perspectives required for the independent social worker. In the MSW Concentration year, the field instructor will encourage the student to make independent choices in professional practice and review those practices in supervisory sessions. The necessary step in this review is the evaluation. At all points of all levels of social work practicum experiences, field instructors should ask themselves and their students whether the learning that is happening is appropriate for the specific stage of professional development. In addition, field instructors should consider questions such as the following: Where can the student be praised for a job well done? Where should the student be encouraged to take on more responsibility? Where is corrective action necessary?

The second thorny factor to consider in conducting the field evaluation is the "student response to evaluation" (Bogo et al., 2007, p. 111). Perhaps the most gratifying and easiest evaluation to conduct involves eager, enthusiastic students who perform all assigned tasks to the utmost of their ability. They are the candidates whom many agencies will want to hire, and they can be very easy to evaluate. Of course, as you give them positive feedback, it is important to be specific. What about the student performance was excellent? Are there blind spots that may impede student progress? These blind spots might include a tendency toward implicit bias or stereotyping certain individuals or groups of individuals. There might also be blind spots regarding client aptitude or attitude toward services or self-sufficiency.

The more difficult situations arise when the student is not performing to agency and field instructor expectations. Most students will have areas where they need to improve. When students need to improve it is important to give clear, specific feedback about those areas. For example, a Foundation student may have difficulty with pacing, that is, allowing clients to fully develop and recount their stories. Or, students may have trouble practicing empathy and the appropriate response to the emotional situation before jumping in with a social work solution. Other students might have problems with documenting their work with clients in a timely manner. Some Concentration-level students are very good at the "behind-the-scenes" work, but hesitate to take leadership in more public settings, such as speaking in front of a group. In each of these cases, students may be unaware or unsure of how to change their behavior or practice. If you have reviewed such issues with a student in the weekly supervision sessions, and the behavior or practice persists, the evaluation will reflect that the student has work to do to improve this area of practice. In those instances, you could use the evaluation opportunity as the "teachable moment" and help the student deconstruct his or her practice. Whatever the behavior or skill, take the necessary time with the student to "unpack" the behavior. What is the obstacle that prevents the successful practice of certain skills or behaviors? What can the student do to improve performance? What specific steps will be useful? If you suspect that there are value conflicts at play, how can you explore those values with the student?

Engaging with students regarding assessment is useful if students can provide an accurate assessment of their current level of performance. Having students complete the evaluation form can point out differences and similarities between their perceptions and those of the field instructor. As a field instructor, you can provide concrete examples of how you perceive the student's work. Sometimes students have an inflated sense of what they have accomplished. Students may be truly bewildered when told that their actions are not suitable for social work practice—for example, bringing a client a gift or bringing meals to a client's home. You can provide students with clear indications of where they have fallen short of expectations.

Giving negative feedback can be unpleasant. Indeed, Munson (2002) suggests that social work supervisors dislike criticism (both giving and receiving it). Situations may arise where the student is unable or unwilling to change his or her practice to reflect necessary improvement. In those situations, the field instructor is obligated to report this to the school, via the evaluation, so that the school can take the necessary next steps. If the student fails the entire placement, this will have implications for the student's pathway to the profession. The school could choose to mediate with you and the student to find a way to suitably address the behaviors and pave the way to the successful achievement of social work skills.

Sometimes, however, the student and the agency are unable to find a successful point of reconciliation. Sometimes this happens after repeated supervisory interventions have occurred and the student has not conformed to agency expectations. Other instances may arise where the student has engaged in unethical practice, to the extent that the behavior is so egregious that immediate action must be taken. In those instances, you and the school faculty field liaison may decide that the student has failed the placement. If this happens, the school must address the behaviors with the student, and provide alternatives. These alternatives may include conditions for continuation during a probationary period, including another field placement. In more extreme cases, alternatives can include the student's withdrawal or dismissal from the program. In any case, this decision is left up to the school.

A third complicating factor in field assessment is the relationship between the field instructor and the student (Bogo et al., 2007). It's possible that you and the student will not work well together. You might have different work styles. Social work supervisors may feel uncomfortable with the power differential between their role and that of the student. This can be particularly true if you, as the field instructor, are not very experienced. Indeed, the role of evaluation can be complicated by the nature of the mentoring relationship. If your role as field instructor is not clear to the student, it may unnecessarily confuse the relationship. The presence of dual relationships can be a consideration in any supervisory interaction. This can happen if the student's field placement is at the student's place of employment, or if the student and the supervisor have known each other before the supervisory relationship was initiated.

As in all supervisory relationships, it is helpful to have a clear understanding about the expectations for supervision sessions, check-in, and assessment. The learning contract, which incorporates valuable aspects of assessment, will provide a great chance to review these expectations of supervision. Having a routine schedule for supervision makes the student evaluation more relevant. You want to assure the student that your feedback is important so that the student takes it seriously. It is important to give feedback early and often. It is a good idea to "connect the dots" and help the student understand and use the learning assessment plan as his or her guide for the field placement. The student and you, the fieldwork supervisor, can refer to the learning contract/assessment plan during each supervision session to make sure that the student is on track toward achieving his or her educational goals.

Finally, consider the organizational context. The agency context can present a considerably difficult factor in view of the different lenses and expectations regarding student behavior and supervision. For example, does the agency respect and value the student's contributions? Does the agency allow you sufficient time to provide meaningful supervision? By extension, does the agency give you sufficient time to adequately supervise and know the student's practice? Are you able to incorporate the student into the day-to-day routine of the agency's business?

WHAT ARE THE OUTCOMES?

Reflective practice is an important skill for any social worker (Knott & Scragg, 2010). As a field instructor, you can model this skill in practice with the student, using the field evaluation form as a key component for reflection. In your exploration of reflective practice, you can model this in the supervisory session. When things don't go according to plan, students can benefit from questions that assess what they could do differently. You can use the evaluation process to facilitate students' plans for future practice. You can also use reflective practice in your work as a field instructor. As field instructor, your efforts can provide the mechanism for maximizing the student's learning and development as a professional. Most important, you can regard the academic environment as your support in making supervisory decisions. Together you can make a powerful learning experience for the student. And, you can make a difference by developing the social work profession of the future.

REFERENCES

Bogo, M., Regehr, C., Power, R., & Regehr, G. (2007). When values collide: Field instructors' experiences of providing feedback and evaluating competence. *The Clinical Supervisor, 26*(1/2), 99–117.

Chui, E. (2010). Desirability and feasibility in evaluating fieldwork performance: Tensions between supervisors and students. *Social Work Education, 29*(2), 171–187.

Cleak, H., Hawkins, L., Laughton, J., & Williams, J. (2015). Creating a standardized teaching and learning framework for social work field placements. *Australian Social Work, 68*(1), 49–64.

Council on Social Work Education. (2008). *Educational policy and accreditation standards.* Alexandria, VA: Author.

Council on Social Work Education. (2010). *Advanced social work practice in clinical social work.* Alexandria, VA: Author.

Everett, J., Miehls, D., DuBois, C., & Garran, A. (2011). The developmental model of supervision as reflected in the experiences of field supervisors and graduate students. *Journal of Teaching in Social Work, 31*(3), 250–264.

Homonoff, E. (2008). The heart of social work: Best practitioners rise to challenges in field instruction. *The Clinical Supervisor, 27*(2), 135–169.

Knight, C. (1996). A study of MSW and BSW students' perceptions of their field instructors. *Journal of Social Work Education, 32*(3), 399–414.

Knott, C., & Scragg, T. (2010). *Reflective practice in social work* (2nd ed.). Exeter, England: Learning Matters.

Munson, D. (2002). *Handbook of clinical social work supervision* (3rd ed.). Binghamton, NY: Haworth Press.

National Association of Social Workers. (2013). *Best practice standards in social work supervision.* Washington, DC: Author.

Peleg-Oren, N., Macgowan, M., & Even-Zahav, R. (2007). Field instructors' commitment to student supervision: Testing the investment model. *Social Work Education, 26*(7), 684–696.

Regehr, G., Bogo, M., Regehr, C., & Power, R. (2007). Can we build a better mousetrap? Improving the measures of practice performance in the field practicum. *Journal of Social Work Education, 43*(2), 327–343.

Tsui, M. (2005). *Social work supervision: Contexts and concepts.* Thousand Oaks, CA: Sage.

Wayne, J., Bogo, M., & Raskin, M. (2010). Field education as the signature pedagogy of social work education. *Journal of Social Work Education, 46*(3), 327–339.

NINE

Field Education and Professional Ethics

Melissa A. Hensley

One of the most important areas of practice that field instructors discuss with their students is teaching and reinforcing the ethics and values of the social work profession (Reamer, 2012). Students are introduced to the *Code of Ethics* of the National Association of Social Workers (NASW) early in their social work education, but it is up to academic faculty and also field instructors to ensure that social work students can make connections between the content of the ethical code and real-life practice situations. In some instances, the *Code of Ethics* may provide clear instruction on the action that should be taken, although in other cases the "correct" decision may not be evident, or there may be more than one alternative that the student could take. Part of learning to make ethical decisions "on the ground" also involves understanding the utility of particular decision-making frameworks when ethical dilemmas arise. Ongoing dialogue between the practicum student and the field instructor on the topic of professional values and ethics is indispensable; in fact, a recent study of students' field education experiences indicated that teaching and learning about social work ethics was one of the most important aspects of the practicum experience, helping students to transition "from *social work student* to *professional social worker*" (Williamson, Hostetter, Byers, & Huggins, 2010, p. 239, emphasis in original).

BACKGROUND

Discussions of the NASW *Code of Ethics* and ways to deal with ethical dilemmas, such as boundary concerns, are topics broached in almost all field instruction textbooks for social work students (for example, Royse, Dhopper, & Rompf, 2012; Ward & Mama, 2010). Surprisingly, however, little empirical research has been conducted on the teaching of ethics in field education (Mathews, Weinger, & Wijnberg, 1997). The existence of the *Journal of Social Work Values and Ethics*, an online journal, has opened the door for more research and discussion of issues related to teaching social work ethics in field education.

The NASW *Code of Ethics* is the primary source for U.S. social work professionals seeking guidance on ethical dilemmas or challenges (NASW, 2008). It is standard practice for many faculty members and field instructors to call upon the *Code of Ethics* when teaching about professional ethics. The International Federation of Social Workers (IFSW) *Statement of Ethical Principles* is also frequently referenced in social work education (IFSW, 2012). Many social work organizations use a variety of ethical decision-making frameworks to guide practice, usually frameworks that are extensively informed by the NASW *Code*. The NASW Minnesota Chapter uses a model called "ETHICS[2]" that outlines a step-by-step process for ethical decision making, using the NASW *Code* and other ethics references as guides (NASW Minnesota, n.d.).

However, other scholars and practitioners have noted that additional models for ethical decision making exist. Mathews et al. (1997) discuss the competing values model as another way to guide decisions involving professional ethics. This model, developed initially by Fleck-Henderson (1991) and informed by theory in social psychology, outlines five decision-making steps: constructing a moral dilemma; addressing the question of responsibility; resolving the dilemma, "not necessarily by reaching a clear decision, but by identifying the focus of control as being intrapsychic, interpersonal, or environmental, or some combination of the three" (Mathews et al., 1997, p. 107); acting upon the dilemma; and justifying the action.

It is important for students to understand the history, context, and expectations involved in common ethical challenges, as well as to have some knowledge of decision-making frameworks that can be used when ethical dilemmas arise.

COMMON ETHICAL CHALLENGES

There are a number of topics that frequently arise as ethical challenges in the practicum. These include mandated reporter responsibilities, mental health treatment and involuntary commitment, worker–client boundaries, specific boundary concerns related to self-disclosure, and disclosure of student status. Another important concern in field instruction is the social work value of cultural responsiveness and its relation to social justice (NASW, 2008). Students will learn about and discuss these issues in their practice methods courses. Field instructors can greatly enhance students' learning by also addressing ethical challenges directly in field supervision.

Mandated Reporter Responsibilities

All states have statutes that require professionals in health care and human services to report suspected incidents of child abuse and neglect. Social workers are considered to be "mandated reporters" of suspected abuse and neglect under these laws. Students are frequently fearful of the responsibility of being a mandated reporter, yet this is an important component of many areas of social work practice. Particularly in practicum settings involving work with children and families, it is important for the field instructor to discuss in detail with the student the circumstances under which a report would need to be made, and the procedure, if any, for informing families that a report has been made (Royse et al., 2012). Teaching students about mandated reporting should include discussion of relevant state laws as well as the policies of the specific agency.

> **Case Example:** Jan, a foundation-year master's degree in social
> work (MSW) student, was working as a practicum student in
> a public elementary school in an urban area. One morning, as
> Jan was facilitating a girls' discussion group, one of her group
> members mentioned that she was afraid of her brother. The
> group member, an 8-year-old Caucasian girl, stated that her
> brother frequently hit her and that he also took food away from
> her at mealtimes. From the group member's report, it appeared
> to Jan that the girl's mother, a single parent, was not intervening
> to help her daughter. Jan had heard from teachers at the school
> that contacting Child Protective Services by calling the Child
> Abuse Hotline only made things worse, and Jan was afraid that
> if she called the hotline, other faculty and staff would criticize
> her, even though the girl in her group had visible bruises. How-
> ever, Jan discussed her concerns with her field instructor. Jan's
> field instructor educated Jan about the details of the state law
> concerning reports of suspected child maltreatment. Jan came to
> the conclusion that it was her responsibility to contact the hot-
> line. Jan's field instructor sat with Jan as she made the call to the
> hotline, in case Jan experienced anxiety or did not know what to
> say. The children's services department for the county was able
> to work with the girl, her brother, and her mother to address the
> young boy's problem behaviors and enhance the mother's par-
> enting skills.

Mandated reporting also can involve reports of abuse or neglect of vulnerable adults (U.S. Department of Health and Human Services, 2014). Vulnerable adults could include older adults, especially those who have dementia or other cognitive impairment. The definition of "vulnerable adult" could also include adults with developmental or psychiatric disabilities who are not considered to have the necessary cognitive skills to make decisions on their own behalf (Minnesota Department of Human Services, 2014). Students should be trained in the definition of "vulnerable adult" in the state in which they are practicing, as well as in the warning signs of elder or vulnerable adult abuse.

Mental Health Treatment and Involuntary Commitment

Many mental health agencies that host practicum students have clients in agency programs who are participating due to a court order mandating mental health treatment. Other agency settings that may have involuntary clients include corrections agencies, addictions treatment programs, juvenile justice programs, and residential treatment programs for children and youth.

If a student will be working with involuntary clients, the student will need instruction in the process by which individuals become involuntary clients and the requisite paperwork associated with documenting clients' participation in agency services. Students should also receive training on how to establish rapport and set treatment goals with involuntary clients (Rooney, 2009). The power dynamic inherent in working with involuntary clients is something that should be explored with practicum students. Too often, involuntary clients are treated disrespectfully, and their choices and preferences are disregarded. A client's involuntary status does not negate the client's right to respectful treatment or the client's right to have input into the treatment process.

Another common ethical struggle related to involuntary treatment is the legitimacy of the entire concept of involuntary treatment. Some mental health advocates have expressed strong views in opposition of involuntary treatment laws (Chamberlin, 1996). Students often struggle with the ethical obligation to keep people safe and the right of clients to self-determination (NASW, 2008). This is a struggle that is worth discussion and processing in students' supervision. Mental Health America offers useful background on policies in its position paper on involuntary treatment (Mental Health America, 2015). White (2013) uses a public health ethical framework to discuss the ethics of involuntary hospitalization.

One helpful way to discuss the ethical challenge of working with involuntary clients is to encourage students to find ways to build alliances with clients regardless of their legal status. Although the power differential between provider and client cannot be dissolved, students can learn to interact with involuntary clients in ways that are empathetic and helpful (Ward & Mama, 2010). Showing empathy toward clients who are not willing participants in treatment can facilitate trust. Frameworks such as the transtheoretical model of change can offer helpful ways for students to collaborate with involuntary clients and help establish mutually agreeable goals (Connors, Donovan, & DiClemente, 2001).

Worker–Client Boundaries

The topic of establishing appropriate professional boundaries is an ethical issue that arises frequently, in many different agency contexts (Ward & Mama, 2010). The issue of boundaries can be especially touchy because many social work students feel uncomfortable with having "power over" their clients, and they may seek to equalize the relationship between themselves and their clients. Students may seek to establish greater comfort in their communications with clients by telling clients details of their life outside the agency.

Nonetheless, it is essential for students to recognize the necessity of healthy professional boundaries. Establishing clear roles and responsibilities for practitioners as well as clients protects the safety of the client and also helps to clarify the expectations of each party in the social worker–client relationship.

Because the social worker–client relationship can have a very "artificial" feel to clients, especially those without much experience in working with helping agencies, clients may not understand what is meant by "healthy boundaries." Clients may act in ways that cross boundaries not because they are being non compliant, but rather because they do not have an understanding of the roles played by helping professionals. Students need a detailed understanding of appropriate boundaries so that they can maintain those boundaries and also explain their role to clients in a compassionate and clear way (NASW, 2008). Providing specific examples of potential boundary violations can be helpful in understanding how these situations can be averted or avoided (Ward & Mama, 2010). Ward and Mama (2010) provide excellent examples of potential situations and ways that students can consult with their field instructors to address these concerns.

Certainly, students should be encouraged to be authentic with clients and to share decision making with clients. However, it is also important for students to understand when "friendliness" or "authenticity" might be crossing the line into inappropriate behavior. Field instructors will want to review the provisions in the NASW *Code of Ethics* that discuss worker–client boundaries, in addition to discussing the policies and expectations of the specific agency setting regarding worker–client relationships. Something as simple as using one's personal vehicle to transport clients may be viewed as standard procedure in one agency, but be forbidden in another. The overall organizational structure may affect perceptions of appropriate boundaries as well. A small drop-in center program may have different agency-level expectations of worker–client relationships than a large clinic or inpatient facility.

Disclosure of Student Status

One particularly troubling ethical challenge can happen when students are instructed not to tell their clients that they are in training. In the practicum process, students should always be forthright with clients and their families about their student status (NASW, 2008). It is inappropriate for a field instructor or other agency staff person to encourage students to hide their student status. Sometimes agency staff members fear that clients and client families will be reluctant to work with students or will not trust students with necessary information about their situation. In other cases, agencies try to make up for staff shortages by asking students to "fill in" as therapists or case managers. It is never appropriate to use students as a cheap substitute for full-time workers, and if clients are reluctant to work with students, they should have a choice. You, as the field instructor, have a responsibility to ensure that clients are well-served and that students who are working with clients have the necessary skills as well as professional support for their learning activities.

Generally speaking, clients are willing to work with students, provided that students have received adequate training and are being well-supervised and supported in their role. Some clients even enjoy working with students and may feel a sense of pride in their role in teaching "the next generation" of social workers. Providing accurate information to clients about the training and experience of students who work with them is an absolute necessity, however.

Other Self-Disclosure Concerns

Students who come into the field of social work frequently have had experiences as consumers of health, mental health, and social services. These experiences often are a motivating factor for an individual to pursue a career in social work. "Lived experience," as it is often called, can enhance a practitioner's level of empathy and provide a sense of passion to the practitioner's work. Care must be taken, however, to ensure that students understand the impact of their lived experience on their practice. Many students experience difficult emotional triggers; this can be especially troubling for students with their own personal history of being a consumer of services (Royse et al., 2012). Field instructors as well as field faculty liaisons can work to help students integrate their experience in a constructive way.

Self-disclosure can be one important piece to consider. In less formal organizational settings, a provider's disclosure of his or her own experience of challenges and recovery may be appropriate, and in some settings, such as some addictions treatment programs, even expected. However, the field instructor and student should always keep in mind that self-disclosure, when it is done, should happen in order to facilitate the patient's trust and progress in treatment, not to provide an opportunity for the student to "vent."

Cultural Responsiveness

Cultural responsiveness in practice is an expectation of the NASW *Code of Ethics* (2008), as well as an essential competency in the Council on Social Work Education's Educational Policy and Accreditation Standards (Council on Social Work Education [CSWE], 2008). The process of teaching skills of cultural responsiveness during the practicum experience may vary greatly depending on the practicum setting. Students may not have complete, up-to-date knowledge of the cultural background of every client with whom they work, but it is important for the field instructor to help students acquire some basic understanding of respectful communication styles that they can use when meeting with clients. In addition, a basic repertoire of respectful communication skills, as well as openness to clients' own wisdom and experience, can be modeled for practicum students.

The Substance Abuse and Mental Health Services Administration (SAMHSA) provides a helpful definition of cultural competence in practice:

> While people often think of culture in terms of race or ethnicity there are many other elements—some that are easy to see and others that are hidden. Cultural competence means being respectful and responsive to the health beliefs, practices, and cultural and linguistic needs of diverse population groups. Lastly, developing cultural competence is an evolving, dynamic process that takes time and occurs along a continuum. (SAMHSA, n.d.)

As the SAMHSA definition points out, cultural responsiveness may involve beliefs and behaviors associated with a particular racial or ethnic group, but it may also involve other cultural elements related to gender, sexual orientation, gender identity, ability status, or other social identities.

Because cultural competency is considered to be an ethical obligation for social work practitioners, this is a topic that should be frequently included in supervision discussions. Field instructors can encourage students to discuss material learned in human behavior and social policy courses in supervision. With some guidance, students can make many important connections between concepts learned in class—such as power and privilege, the impact of social identity, and social justice—with situations that they are experiencing in the field.

> **Case Example:** Anna, a 20-year-old, European American junior-
> year bachelor's degree in social work (BSW) student, had
> started a practicum at Healing Communities, an HIV/AIDS
> service organization. Anna's father identified as a gay man,
> and Anna knew that many of her father's friends had been af-
> fected directly or indirectly by the HIV/AIDS epidemic. One of
> Anna's first activities at Healing Communities was to observe
> a support group for people living with HIV, in preparation for
> becoming a group co-facilitator. Anna shared with Todd, her
> supervisor, that she felt well prepared to sit in on this group be-
> cause she "understood what people were going through." She
> anticipated a group predominantly composed of middle-class,
> White gay men. When Anna attended the group, however, she
> was surprised to find that the racial/ethnic composition of the
> group was much more diverse, with participants who identified
> as non-Hispanic White, Latino, and African American. Although
> group members did discuss experiences of discrimination based
> on their HIV status, much of the group revolved around main-
> taining positive mental and physical health, as well as ensuring
> adherence to the medical treatments that would help keep them
> healthy. Anna shared with Todd that this was a good, but sur-
> prising learning experience for her, which challenged some of
> her assumptions. Anna felt better able to transition into the role

of co-facilitator, as she had gained a greater capacity to listen and learn rather than enter the group with her own conceptions of what group members needed.

In addition, students should not assume that they do not have to be concerned with cultural responsiveness in situations where their outward social identity appears similar to that of clients they may be working with. Even when a social work practitioner appears to have much in common with a client, the process of getting to know the client as an individual and understanding that client's own experiences and characteristics is essential (Williamson et al., 2010).

COMPETENCE IN PRACTICE

Neither practicing social workers nor social work students should enter into the process of delivering services that they are not competent to deliver (NASW, 2008). If a student is being asked to participate in the delivery of a particular treatment or practice method, he or she needs training and supervision appropriate to the practice method. This training may involve lectures and formal training sessions, as well as shadowing an experienced practitioner as he or she works with clients. Students need ongoing mentoring as they learn new practice methods, whether those methods involve clinical intervention techniques or macro-practice approaches. A "sink-or-swim" approach to learning new practice techniques, in which the student is given practice tasks with no training or orientation, is never wise (Cimino, Rorke, & Adams, 2013).

ETHICAL DILEMMAS

In addition to the decision-making strategies discussed in the introduction to this chapter, there are a number of other approaches to resolving ethical dilemmas. Scott, Boylan, and Jungers (2015) suggest the use of principle-based ethics and virtue ethics.

Regardless of the philosophy or theoretical framework used in approaching an ethical dilemma, students should always be encouraged to discuss ethical concerns and dilemmas with the field instructor or other professional colleagues. Feedback from professional peers can help improve the quality of decision making and enable the student to consider a variety of perspectives (Gough & Spencer, 2014).

Principle-Based Ethics

A decision-making process that uses principle-based ethics relies on certain basic ethical principles or obligations as a guide to determining the best course of action. Common principles used in this process include beneficence (the value of doing good toward others), respect for autonomy (recognizing the validity of other people's choices and priorities), and justice (treating people equally), among others. Examining these principles and the priority that they take in the decision-making process can be helpful at times when a professional code of ethics does not provide a clear-cut solution (Scott et al., 2015).

Reviewing the basic tenets of principle-based ethics with students is an important learning experience. Having a discussion with students about the relative priority of different ethical principles in the specific agency setting can be helpful as well. Although many social workers would likely agree about the importance of the various principles, using the principles to help resolve ethical dilemmas could look different from one agency to the next, based on the mission and client/ stakeholder base of the organization (Scott et al., 2015).

Virtue Ethics

Virtue ethics differ from principle-based ethics in that they focus on the personal traits or character of the person who is making the decision. Personality factors associated with social work include such things as "professional wisdom, care, respectfulness, and courage" (Pullen-Sansfacon, 2010, p. 403). It is believed that developing virtuous qualities in oneself will enhance the capacity for ethical decision making. Using virtue ethics can align well with the acquisition of social work competencies that emphasize professional identity and self-knowledge (CSWE, 2008).

Although models of decision making based on virtue ethics are used less frequently in social work than principle-based models, virtue ethics can be applied to social work practice situations (Scott et al., 2015). Virtue-based decision making places a high value on self-reflection and a character trait known as "practical reasoning" (Pullen-Sansfacon, 2010, p. 405). In work with students, field instructors can assist students in developing habits of reflective practice (Kottler & Jones, 2003), which can inform decision making when a particular code of ethics does not provide clear guidance.

CONCLUSION

Education regarding professional ethics should be infused throughout the entire practicum experience. Students should receive "upfront" training about organizational expectations in their orientation to the practicum and the agency. In addition, the supervisory setting should be a place where students can bring ethical questions on an ongoing basis (Danowski, 2012). Specific issues that frequently arise in the practicum agency should be addressed by the field instructor, and the field instructor should also encourage students to bring their questions and dilemmas into supervision for discussion. Several models exist to help students determine an ethical course of action or to resolve an ethical dilemma. Practicing as an ethical social worker requires not only knowledge of the NASW *Code of Ethics*, but also the ability to apply sound decision-making strategies to everyday situations encountered in social work practice.

ACKNOWLEDGMENT

Nancy Rodenborg, PhD, LGSW, assisted with fine-tuning this chapter and helped the author better understand cultural competence as an ethical obligation of the social work profession.

REFERENCES

Chamberlin, J. (1996). *Citizenship rights and psychiatric disability.* Retrieved September 19, 2015, from https://www.power2u.org/articles/empower/citizenship.html

Cimino, A. N., Rorke, J., & Adams, H. L. (2013). Supervisors behaving badly: Witnessing ethical dilemmas and what to do about it. *Journal of Social Work Values and Ethics, 10*(2), 48–57.

Connors, G. J., Donovan, D. M., & DiClemente, C. C. (2001). *Substance abuse treatment and the stages of change: Selecting and planning interventions.* New York, NY: Guilford.

Council on Social Work Education. (2008). *Educational policy and accreditation standards.* Alexandria, VA: Author.

Danowski, W. A. (2012). *In the field: A guide for the social work practicum* (2nd ed.). Boston, MA: Pearson Education.

Fleck-Henderson, A. (1991). Moral reasoning in social work practice. *Social Service Review, 65*(2), 185–202.

Gough, J., & Spencer, E. (2014). Ethics in action: An exploratory survey of social workers' ethical decision making and value conflicts. *Journal of Social Work Values and Ethics, 11*(2), 23–40.

International Federation of Social Workers. (2012). *Statement of ethical principles.* Retrieved June 12, 2015, from http://ifsw.org/policies/statement-of-ethical-principles/

Kottler, J. A., & Jones, W. P. (2003). *Doing better: Improving clinical skills and professional competence.* New York, NY: Brunner-Routledge.

Matthews, G., Weinger, S., & Wijnberg, M. (1997). Ethics in field education: Promise, pretension, or practice? *Journal of Sociology and Social Welfare, 24*(2), 103–115.

Mental Health America. (2015). *Position statement 22: Involuntary treatment.* Retrieved June 12, 2015, from http://www.mentalhealthamerica.net/positions/involuntary-treatment

Minnesota Department of Human Services. (2014). *Adult protection.* Retrieved March 16, 2014, from http://mn.gov/dhs/people-we-serve/seniors/services/adult-protection/

National Association of Social Workers. (2008). *Code of ethics of the National Association of Social Workers.* Retrieved March 14, 2015, from http://www.naswdc.org/pubs/code/code.asp

National Association of Social Workers Minnesota. (n.d.). *Case discussion reporting form.* St. Paul, MN: Author.

Pullen-Sansfacon, A. (2010). Virtue ethics for social work: A new pedagogy for practical reasoning. *Social Work Education, 29*(4), 402–415.

Reamer, F. (2012). Essential ethics education in social work field education. *Field Educator, 2*(2). Retrieved March 14, 2015, from http://www.fieldeducator.simmons.edu/article/essential-ethics-education-in-social-work-field-instruction

Rooney, R. H. (Ed.). (2009). *Strategies for work with involuntary clients* (2nd ed.). New York, NY: Columbia University Press.

Royse, D., Dhopper, S. S., & Rompf, E. L. (2012). *Field instruction: A guide for social work students* (Updated ed.). Boston, MA: Pearson Education.

Scott, J., Boylan, J. C., & Jungers, C. M. (2015). *Practicum and internship: Textbook and resource guide for counseling and psychotherapy* (5th ed.). New York, NY: Routledge.

Substance Abuse and Mental Health Services Administration. (n.d.). *Cultural competence.* Retrieved June 12, 2015, from https://captus.samhsa.gov/prevention-practice/ strategic-prevention-framework/cultural-competence

U.S. Department of Health and Human Services, Administration for Community Living. (2014). *What is elder abuse?* Retrieved June 12, 2015, from http://www.aoa .gov/AoA_programs/elder_rights/EA_prevention/whatisEA.aspx

Ward, K., & Mama, R. S. (2010). *Breaking out of the box: Adventure-based field instruction.* Chicago, IL: Lyceum.

White, E. (2013). The ethics of involuntary hospitalization. *Journal of Social Work Values and Ethics, 10*(2), 25–35.

Williamson, S., Hostetter, C., Byers, K., & Huggins, P. (2010, Fall). I found myself at this practicum: Student reflections on field education. *Advances in Social Work, 11*(2), 235–247.

Conclusion

Melissa A. Hensley

Serving as a field instructor can be one of the most rewarding experiences of a social worker's practice. Working with students and watching as they develop from novices into skilled, thoughtful practitioners is rewarding on many levels.

To ensure that you and your practicum students are able to make the most of the field experience, it is important to understand the purpose of field education, as well as the responsibilities of the field instructor and student (Lotmore, 2014). Field education provides a place and time for social work knowledge and values to come together with day-to-day practice tasks. Activities in the practicum setting enable students to learn practice techniques and understand how they relate to the client's needs and goals, as well as the mission of the practicum organization.

As the field instructor, you are responsible for providing an agency setting in which social work students can integrate classroom learning, apply professional ethics to practice, and master a variety of practice skills. The guidance you provide to students as they develop their learning agendas and put their learning goals into action is indispensable. From regular face-to-face supervision to timely feedback on the performance of learning activities, you are helping your student to develop into a capable professional.

Your student should come to the practicum with an open mind and a willingness to learn new knowledge and skills. You, also, should approach the practicum with an open mind as well as the willingness to learn from your student. You and your student should both have a commitment to regular supervision, and your student should come to supervisory sessions with relevant questions or feedback related to the practicum experience.

As you work with your students to integrate knowledge from the classroom into the work of the practicum, you can assist students in understanding ways that the intentional integration of various theoretical perspectives can guide practice. Whether you use a structured, systematic approach or integrate theory discussions into ongoing supervision meetings, the task of applying theory to the day-to-day practice of social work is a critical part of the practicum learning experience.

Assessment of performance in the practicum begins with the construction of a thoughtful learning agenda and continues through midterm and final evaluation meetings. The feedback you provide to students is indispensable in helping them to polish their skills and develop increased self-awareness. Field assessment does indeed help students to adopt the social work value of lifelong learning (National Association of Social Workers, 2008).

The field instructor role is sometimes taken for granted. Without the affiliation of many skilled social workers with academic social work schools and departments, schools of social work would not be able to supply the community with graduates who are adequately prepared for multiple levels of social work practice. We hope that this "survival guide" helps you fulfill your role as a field educator more effectively, and that you can use the helpful hints in this volume to grow in your own professional development.

REFERENCES

Lotmore, A. (2014). Whos, whats, and hows of being a successful social work field supervisor. *The New Social Worker, 21*(1), 6–7.

National Association of Social Workers. (2008). *Code of ethics of the National Association of Social Workers.* Retrieved March 14, 2015, from http://www.naswdc.org/pubs/code/code.asp

Resources for Inquisitive Field Instructors

WHERE CAN I GO TO LEARN MORE ABOUT TEACHING TECHNIQUES?

Carnegie Foundation for the Advancement of Teaching
www.carnegiefoundation.org
(Research, blogs, and commentary on liberal arts and professional education)

Faculty Focus
www.facultyfocus.com
(Resources related to instructional techniques in higher education)

National Mental Health Consumers' Self-Help Clearinghouse
www.mhselfhelp.org
(Information on wellness and recovery practices and resources for teaching about client empowerment)

WHERE CAN I GO TO LEARN MORE ABOUT SOCIAL WORK FIELD INSTRUCTION?

Field Educator
fieldeducator.simmons.edu
(An online social work journal that publishes articles and commentaries related to field education)

National Association of Social Workers, Practice Web Page
www.naswdc.org/practice/default.asp
(Definitions of social work practice and of scope of practice in different areas; information about social work skills and competencies)

Social Work Today
www.socialworktoday.com
(A magazine for practitioners that regularly features articles on field instruction)

The New Social Worker
www.socialworker.com
(Articles written by instructors and students related to social work education, field instruction, and professional practice)

WHERE CAN I GO TO LEARN MORE ABOUT EVIDENCE-BASED PRACTICE IN SOCIAL WORK?

Council on Social Work Education
www.cswe.org/CentersInitiatives/CurriculumResources/Teaching
Evidence-BasedPractice.aspx
(Examples of evidence-based practice processes and sample syllabi)

Macro-Practice Skills

sowkweb.usc.edu/download/msw/field-education/copa-macro-practice-skills
(List of macro-practice skills relevant to social work students at all levels)

National Registry of Evidence-Based Programs and Practices

www.samhsa.gov/nrepp
(Information on evidence-based practices in mental health and substance use treatment)

Social Work Policy Institute

www.socialworkpolicy.org/research/evidence-based-practice-2.html
(Examples of registries and other resources for promoting EBP)

Resources for Policy Practice

Children's Defense Fund
www.childrensdefense.org
(A national advocacy organization for issues related to children, especially children in poverty and children/families in the child welfare system)

Child Welfare League of America
www.cwla.org
(A coalition of organizations working in child welfare policy and practice)

Kaiser Family Foundation
kff.org
(A private foundation providing information on health care reform and health care policy)

Mental Health America
www.mentalhealthamerica.net
(A national education and advocacy organization on mental health and mental health treatment)

National Alliance on Mental Illness

www.nami.org

(A national advocacy organization on topics related to mental illness and mental health treatment)

National Association of Social Workers

www.naswdc.org

(A social work professional organization that lobbies on issues related to social work practice and the social work profession)

National Coalition for the Homeless

nationalhomeless.org/advocacy/index.html

(A coalition of organizations advocating for homeless services and homelessness prevention)

Social Welfare Action Alliance

socialwelfareactionalliance.org

(A national organization of progressive human services workers)

Resources for Program Evaluation

Children's Defense Fund Research Library
www.childrensdefense.org/library
(Data and research on programs and services for children)

Evaluation Center
brownschool.wustl.edu/Faculty/ResearchCenters/Evaluation-Center/Pages/default.aspx
(Resources and consultation for program evaluation)

Kids Count Data Center, Annie E. Casey Foundation
datacenter.kidscount.org
(State-by-state data on child and family well-being)

Results-Based Accountability
raguide.org
(Resources and information for the results-based accountability evaluation process)

United States Census Bureau, State & County Quick Facts
quickfacts.census.gov/qfd/index.html
(Census data for use in neighborhood or community assessment)

ACKNOWLEDGMENT

Thanks to Mary Simonson Clark for her contributions to the resource lists in Appendices A, B, and C.

Index